WORLD CUP

MATT CHRISTOPHER®

The #1 Sports Series for Kids

LITTLE, BROWN AND COMPANY

New York • Boston

Little, Brown and Company
Hachette Book Group
1290 Avenue of the Americas, New York, NY 10104
Visit us at LBYR.com

mattchristopher.com

Portions of this book were originally published in 2010.
First Revised Edition: April 2018

Text written by Stephanie True Peters

ISBNs: 978-0-316-48487-9 (pbk.), 978-0-316-48488-6 (ebook)

Printed in the United States of America

LSC-C

10 9 8 7 6 5 4 3 2 1

CONTENTS

WORLD CUP

INTRODUCTION

A GAME FOR THE AGES

In 1894, soccer was poised to join baseball, football, and basketball as one of the most popular sports in the United States. Everything pointed to its success. It had a set of standard rules, just like the others, and it had its own professional league, just like the others. The teams had access to newly constructed baseball stadiums, so finding big venues to play in wasn't a problem. And soccer had a widespread fan base, particularly among European immigrants setting up new lives in the United States. In their countries, soccer was king.

In the United States, however, soccer sank into virtual oblivion while baseball, football, and basketball rose to greatness. Why?

The answer seems to lie in the way the sport was handled. In Europe, soccer clubs were organized and managed by people who loved the game. Here, it was run by the baseball team owners who cared more about making money than they did about promoting soccer itself. When the first professional league failed to turn a profit, these men shut it down to focus on baseball.

While soccer was fading far into the background of the American sports scene, it was spreading like wildfire in many other countries. In fact, it was well on its way to becoming what it is today: the most popular sport on the planet.

The sport Americans call soccer and others call football was born on December 8, 1863, in Great Britain. On that day, a group of eleven English teams formed the London Football Association and published a set of rules by which the sport was to be played. Those rules were adopted by other countries in the coming decades, and while they have been modified since, they have remained essentially the same.

Soccer's roots stretch thousands of years further back in time, however. The oldest known form of the game, *t'su chu*, was played in ancient China as early as 2500 BC. Three thousand years later, the Japanese developed a different version of the game, called *kemari*, which was a combination of modern-day hacky sack and soccer. The ancient Greeks competed in their own kicking game called *episkyros*.

The Romans adopted the Greek sport, which they renamed *harpastum*. Harpastum was very popular with

Roman soldiers. They introduced it to the peoples they conquered during the expansion of the Roman Empire, including those living on the British Isles. The Brits took to it right away—and soccer has been part of British culture, in one form or another, ever since.

The rules set down by the London Football Association in 1863 were quickly accepted by other countries. Soon, soccer blossomed from a club sport into an international phenomenon. To help fuel the fire, seven countries—France, Belgium, Denmark, Switzerland, the Netherlands, Spain, and Sweden—decided to create a governing organization for the sport. They founded the Fédération Internationale de Football Association, or FIFA, in Paris on May 21, 1904. Within the year, England, Scotland, Wales, Ireland, Austria, Hungary, Germany, and Italy had joined FIFA as well.

One of FIFA's first acts was to propose an annual championship tournament among the national teams. It wasn't a new idea. England and Scotland had played each other in just such a competition back in 1872. FIFA's tournament, however, would be on a much grander scale and therefore would, it was hoped, increase international interest in the sport even more.

The proposal was met with great enthusiasm. The inaugural competition was set for 1906.

But that competition never took place. It was canceled for one simple reason: none of the teams sent in applications! In the wake of such a colossal failure, the tournament idea was scrapped, to be revisited at a later date.

As it turned out, that date was much, much later. The 1908 and 1912 Olympics were in part to blame for the delay. After all, the Games included soccer matches between the best teams in the world, so why would another, very similar competition be necessary? Then, from 1914 to 1918, World War I threw many nations into utter chaos. After the war, the 1920 Olympics overshadowed all other international competitions.

In 1924, however, FIFA's new president, Jules Rimet, resurrected the tournament idea. Rimet wanted to turn soccer into an international sports sensation. The tournament was a big part of his plan to reach that goal.

The pieces fell into place soon after the 1924 Olympic soccer competition. The gold-medal winner was Uruguay, which played a fast-paced, thrilling style of soccer that captivated fans and left them clamoring for more. Rimet witnessed that enthusiasm and knew the time was right for FIFA's tournament.

A Uruguayan diplomat named Enrique Buero

agreed. He, too, had seen the crowds cheering for his country's players. At the time, Uruguay was struggling to be accepted into international circles, but soccer had pushed his nation into the limelight as nothing else ever had. Buero realized that if Uruguay hosted FIFA's tournament, the country would gain the attention it needed.

Buero approached Rimet with an offer to hold FIFA's tournament in Uruguay in 1930, his country's one hundredth birthday. Rimet was delighted but cautious. After all, while he wanted the tournament to happen, FIFA hadn't seriously considered the idea for nearly twenty years. And even if the Fédération did decide to hold the competition, there was no guarantee that it would accept Uruguay as the host nation.

The first hurdle was cleared in 1927, when FIFA officially agreed to pursue a world championship. The second hurdle, however, proved more difficult.

In 1929, five other countries expressed interest in playing host. It took all of Rimet's powers of persuasion to convince them to withdraw. When they did, Uruguay was selected as the host of the first FIFA tournament—or "World Cup," as it was already being called.

But selecting a country in which to play soccer and actually *playing* in that country turned out to be two very different things. In 1929, Europe and the United States were wading waist-deep in economic disaster, and most of their players could not afford a journey to South America. The trip to Uruguay was also very time consuming; it would leave many European teams without their best players for two months.

As the date for the World Cup neared, the European teams began pushing for a change of location.

"Hold the World Cup in Rome," they suggested, "and then we'll play."

But by then, plans were already in place for Uruguay to host. Changing the location, with the tournament so near, was not feasible.

Once more Rimet stepped in. He managed to get four European nations—Belgium, France, Romania, and Yugoslavia—to commit to playing in the tournament in Uruguay. With the United States, Mexico, and seven South American countries also on board, that brought the total number of teams competing in the first-ever World Cup to thirteen.

It had taken twenty-four years—or thousands, if you went back in time far enough—but at last, the dream of an international soccer competition was about to come true.

CHAPTER ONE

★ 1930 ★

THE HOST IS THE MOST

On July 15, 1930, Argentina and France met to play the second game of the first World Cup—a match that would go down in soccer history, not because of its exciting action or high score, but because it produced one of the oddest endings to any match ever played.

The teams were equals in every way, leading to a scoreless first half. It wasn't until the eighty-one-minute mark, in fact, that Argentina's Luisito Monti booted the ball into the net. Argentina 1, France 0.

France redoubled its efforts and, as the clock wound down to the final minutes, got within striking range of Argentina's goal. They had just launched their attack when suddenly the referee blew his whistle to signal that the game was over. Time, it seemed, had run out for the French.

Or had it? It turned out that the referee had misread the clock. There were actually six minutes left to play!

Players were called back to the field—some of them out of the locker-room showers—and the game resumed half an hour later. Much to France's disappointment, however, the final result was the same. Argentina defeated them, 1–0.

France's loss came on the second day of the 1930 World Cup. That same week, nine of the thirteen participating teams were forced out of the competition, leaving Yugoslavia, Uruguay, and the United States to join Argentina in the semifinal round.

That two South American teams, Uruguay and Argentina, had made it so far in the competition was no surprise. After all, Uruguay was the reigning Olympic champion and boasted top scorer Pedro Cea. Argentina had offensive might, too, including Luisito Monti and Guillermo Stábile, who was nicknamed El Infiltrador, or "the Infiltrator," for his ability to worm his way past the defense.

The United States, still a newcomer to soccer, had reached the semifinals by literally muscling its way past the competition. Its players were big, but not as skilled as those on other teams. Argentina ran roughshod over them, outscoring the bewildered Americans six goals to one.

Yugoslavia was a surprise team and something

of a mystery to the other nations. No one had seen enough of its style of play to know how it might fare against Uruguay. But how it fared was badly: the host country trounced the Yugoslavs, 6–1.

That victory set the stage for one of the most anticipated and highly charged finals the soccer world had ever known.

Uruguay and Argentina had been rivals on and off the pitch for years. All of South America was watching to see which country would come out on top. Nothing less than national pride was on the line.

In fact, when the Uruguayans found out that Argentina's star player, veteran Pancho Varallo, had a broken foot, they rejoiced in the streets. In response, the Argentine coach ordered Varallo to play despite his injury. To do otherwise, the coach intimated, would make Argentina appear weak.

Eighty thousand fans packed into Centenario Stadium, a brand-new arena built especially for the finals (and completed just days before the match!). Emotions in the stands were running hot—so hot, in fact, that police were ordered to search spectators for weapons in order to prevent violence.

The first World Cup finals began at three thirty on July 30. Within the first minutes, Argentina lost one of its key players when Varallo fell to the ground, writhing in pain from his foot injury.

The loss of Varallo gave Uruguay an instant boost. Twelve minutes into the first half, they attacked the goal. Pablo Dorado got his foot on the ball and kicked. One second later, Uruguay was on the board—and Dorado was in the record books for scoring the first-ever World Cup finals goal.

But Argentina didn't let up. Eight minutes later, Carlos Peucelle answered with a goal for his side. El Infiltrador added a second one for Argentina and in doing so caused the first disagreement of the game. Uruguay claimed that Argentina had been offside—that is, there hadn't been two defenders between the offensive player and the goalie when the shooter received the pass. Therefore, they argued, the goal didn't count.

But the referee stood by his call. The goal stayed on the board.

Argentina went into the second half with a one-point lead over the world champion. They didn't keep that lead for long, however. At the fifty-seven-minute mark, Pedro Cea of Uruguay booted the ball into the net to tie the game. Eleven minutes after that, teammate Santos Iriarte did the same. Now Uruguay had the lead, 3–2!

That was too much for Pancho Varallo to bear. He signaled to his coach that he wanted to go back into the game, pain or no. When he limped onto the field, he did more than change the lineup: he brought new life back to the flagging Argentines, inspiring them to play harder. He himself played as hard as he could despite his injury and, late in the game, very nearly tied the score.

In fact, according to Varallo, he *had* tied the score. Uruguay's goalkeeper, he argued, had knocked one of his shots back *after* it had crossed the goal line. But once again, the referee had the final word on the play. He said the ball had been deflected *before* it crossed the line and, therefore, was not a goal.

Uruguay sealed the win with another goal a minute before the game ended, making the final score Uruguay 4, Argentina 2. The Olympic champs were victorious again!

Raucous celebrations erupted throughout the stadium, in the streets, and throughout the host country. Jules Rimet presented the Victory Cup (renamed the Jules Rimet Cup in 1946) to the Uruguayan Football

Association's president, beginning a tradition that remains unbroken today.

By all accounts, the first World Cup had been a huge triumph for the sport of soccer. The only question now was, how could FIFA build on this success and make the second competition even better?

AP/Wide World Photos

Uruguay in a historic moment: a goal in the first-ever World Cup final

CHAPTER TWO

★ 1934 ★

WELCOME TO ITALY

The first World Cup had seen participation by only thirteen teams. Four years later, despite troubles caused by the crumbling world economy, a total of thirty-two nations sent in applications to take part in the 1934 World Cup.

FIFA was delighted that interest in soccer had grown so dramatically. But a pool of thirty-two teams was simply too large for one event (or so they thought at the time; later on, thirty-two teams would seem just right). So the Fédération decided to hold a series of qualifying rounds to whittle the number of participants down to sixteen. That practice continues on a much larger scale today.

Sadly, one team chose not to take part in the competition at all. Uruguay had felt insulted when some European countries, including Italy, had refused to travel to South America for the 1930 World Cup. When Italy was chosen as the host for 1934, Uruguay withdrew in retaliation.

Uruguay wasn't the only nation dismayed by the choice of Italy. FIFA itself had some serious misgivings about the host. It wasn't the country's ability to hold the tournament that concerned the Fédération, but its leader, Benito Mussolini. Mussolini was a fierce dictator intent on turning Italy into a dominant world power (Mussolini would later side with Adolf Hitler and Nazi Germany during World War II). FIFA feared Mussolini would use the World Cup to promote his goals. But, unfortunately, no other nation stepped forward to play host; it was Italy or nowhere.

Italy welcomed fifteen other national teams to the second World Cup. Twelve of those teams, including the host nation, were from Europe. The remaining four were the United States, Argentina, Brazil, and the first African nation to compete, Egypt.

Play began on May 27 with eight elimination matches taking place in eight different Italian cities. At the end of the day, Italy, Germany, Czechoslovakia, Austria, Spain, Sweden, Switzerland, and Hungary emerged victorious. These eight teams competed in a second elimination round that left Italy, Czechoslovakia, Austria, and Germany standing while the others returned home.

Next up was the semifinal round. The first match

saw Czechoslovakia beating Germany three goals to one. Then came the most anticipated match of the competition between the sport's two biggest powerhouses, Austria and Italy.

Austria used an innovative offense based on short passes, a strategy perfected by its best player, Mathias Sindelar. With Sindelar leading the charge, the Austrian team had won eighteen consecutive games. One of those victories was a 4–2 win over Italy four months earlier. The Austrians entered the match hoping to hand the Italians another defeat.

Italy looked more than able to deny them that satisfaction, however. Thanks to a unique law that allowed people to claim Italian citizenship if they could prove they descended from an Italian family, their roster was stacked with talented imports that included star Luisito Monti as well as fellow Argentine Raimondo Orsi. Leading the charge was coach Vittorio Pozzo, who had single-handedly launched his country's soccer program years earlier.

The Italian team got a break even before the match began. One of Austria's top scorers, Johann Horvath, was sidelined with an injury. As an added bonus, the pitch was a soggy, muddy mess. The field conditions slowed Austria's short-passing game and made Monti's job of disarming Sindelar's attack that much easier.

Italy scored first. The goal came when the ball squeaked past Austria's goalkeeper to reach Italy's Enrico Guaita. All Guaita had to do was knock the ball into the net—which he did.

Try as they might, the Austrians couldn't even things up. After ninety minutes of rough play, Italy was on the way to the finals to face Czechoslovakia.

The game was played on June 10 in Rome in front of a stadium packed with fifty thousand fans, including Benito Mussolini and Jules Rimet. All probably assumed they would see an offensive duel—certainly a possibility, considering Czechoslovakian player Oldřich Nejedlý was the Cup's top scorer so far with five goals, while Angelo Schiavio had three and Orsi two for Italy.

Instead, what they saw was a defensive standoff. After more than seventy minutes, neither team had scored! Then finally, with fourteen minutes remaining, Antonín Puč of Czechoslovakia slipped a low drive past Italian goalkeeper and team captain Giampiero Combi. The Czechs were on the scoreboard and were very close to adding a second goal when one of their shots rebounded off the post.

In the stands, Mussolini sat in stony silence. He was not a soccer fan, but with national pride on the line, he wanted his team to win. According to some, he had made it clear to coach Pozzo that defeat would not be tolerated.

Luckily for Pozzo, Orsi wanted to win just as badly. At the eighty-one-minute mark, he took a shot. And what a shot it was! Rather than sailing on a line, it spiraled weirdly, baffling the Czech goalkeeper, who hesitated for a split second before acting. By then, he was too late: the ball was in the net and the score was tied!

It remained tied through the remaining minutes, forcing a thirty-minute overtime, scheduled to take place the next day. It took just five minutes of that time for Italy's Schiavio to deliver the winning goal. Czechoslovakia couldn't answer. Italy was the World Cup champion!

While the host country celebrated its victory, Rimet began to plan for the third FIFA championship, scheduled to be held in 1938. But even the best-laid plans can go awry. In the years that followed, events began to unfold that would have an impact on soccer—and the world.

CHAPTER THREE

★ 1938 ★

"WIN OR DIE"

When FIFA published the schedule for the 1938 World Cup preliminary matches, Austria was listed among the participating nations. On October 5, 1937, the team beat Latvia to earn one of the sixteen finalist slots.

But when the World Cup began in early June of 1938, Austria was not among the competitors—because Austria no longer existed as a nation. It had been forcibly annexed by Germany three months earlier. The annexation, called the *Anschluss*, had been orchestrated by Germany's dictator, Adolf Hitler, as the first major step toward his goal of world domination.

The unification extended to Austria's and Germany's soccer programs. After the Anschluss, Austria's best players were cherry-picked to strengthen Germany's roster.

One of those players, Matthias Sindelar, refused to accept Hitler's "invitation" to play for Germany, however. He claimed that his decision was based on his age, not his politics. Still, Sindelar made it clear that he opposed Hitler and his agenda. He even went out of his way to greet the former chairman of the Austrian team, who was Jewish, despite being ordered to ignore the man.

"The new chairman has forbidden me to greet you," he said, "but I, Herr Doktor, will always greet you."

Less than a year later, Sindelar was discovered in his apartment, dead from carbon monoxide poisoning. His death was ruled an accident, but rumors have persisted to this day that he was killed for his defiance or that perhaps he committed suicide.

Even without Sindelar, the German squad promised to be a powerhouse in the competition. And that was exactly what Hitler wanted it to be. After all, domination in the world of soccer was a small but significant part of his plan to dominate the world itself.

But Italy's ruler, Benito Mussolini, wasn't about to let Hitler's German team steal the Cup from Italy without a fight. He sent the defending champions to the competition with a three-word message: "Win or die." According to some historians, this message simply meant "do your best to be victorious." Given the political tensions of the time, however, some of the players may have taken the words much more literally.

The third World Cup was held in France. The first round of play began on June 4 with a match between Switzerland and Germany. The game ended in a 1–1 tie, forcing a rematch four days later. That day, the Swiss team bested the German squad decisively, 4–2—despite becoming the first squad in the history of the World Cup to score an "own goal" when they kicked the ball into their own net! With the loss, Hitler's quest to rule the world of soccer ended in failure.

In the meantime, on June 5, France beat Belgium, Hungary annihilated the Dutch East Indies, Italy defeated Norway, the Netherlands fell to Czechoslovakia, and Cuba tied Romania, forcing another rematch. But by far the most exciting game of the first round was between Brazil and Poland.

Brazil was South America's only representative that year. Argentina had qualified, but when Jules Rimet chose France as the host country, the Argentines withdrew in anger. They had been led to believe that the Cup's location would alternate between Europe and the Americas, and they had petitioned hard to play host. Understandably, they were furious that a European nation had been selected for the second time in a row. Other countries from Central and North America, including the United States, sided with Argentina and withdrew after qualifying.

But Brazil's opponent, Poland, was eager to play in its first World Cup. After suffering elimination in the qualifying rounds in 1934, it had fought hard to reach the final competition this year.

The match, held in Strasbourg in driving rain, was an offensive battle from the start. Brazil struck first with a goal off the foot of Leônidas da Silva. Leônidas was nicknamed the "Rubber Man" because of the way he bent around defenses. Among Leônidas's other legendary achievements was the perfection of the bicycle kick, later made famous by another Brazilian—Pelé.

Leônidas's goal came eighteen minutes into the game. But Poland's Fryderyk Scherfke answered five minutes later with a penalty goal to tie the score.

Brazil fought back, chalking up two more goals to end the first half with a satisfying 3–1 lead. That gap shrank eight minutes into the second half, when Ernest Wilimowski of Poland walloped one into the net. The lead disappeared completely six minutes later, when Wilimowski booted in another goal.

Brazil got the upper hand again at the seventy-one-minute mark with a goal by José Perácio, his second of the game. As the clock ticked steadily through the remaining time, they held on to the one-point lead. With one minute left to play, a victory for the South Americans seemed assured.

But then—*whomp!* Wilimowski scored yet *another* goal. Tie score!

With two other tiebreaker matches already scheduled, FIFA decided to continue the game that day. Leônidas came out kicking, delivering two goals in quick succession to put Brazil ahead and earn him a hat trick (three goals in one game).

Poland couldn't recover, although Wilimowski did what no player had yet to do in a World Cup, namely, score four goals in one game. His fourth and final goal came with less than two minutes remaining. It was a fantastic achievement, but just not enough. Final score: Brazil 6, Poland 5.

After such excitement early on in the competition, the games that followed were something of a letdown—particularly for Czechoslovakia, which lost to Brazil in a second round tiebreaker, and Cuba, which lost to Sweden, 8–0. One by one, other teams fell, too, until only Italy and Hungary remained.

From the start, the Italians were the heavy favorites. Not only had they taken the World Cup in 1934 but were also the gold-medal winners of the 1936 Olympics. Their players, coached by veteran Vittorio Pozzo, had several years of experience under their belts. They knew one another's style of play and they knew how to pick apart their opposition.

In the final match, they put that experience and knowledge to work right away with a goal by Gino Colaussi on an assist by Giuseppe Meazza. Meazza was a stellar player, a "born forward" according to Pozzo, and the team's captain. He was also cool as a cucumber in stressful situations, as evidenced by one of the more memorable moments of the 1938 World Cup.

Midway through the semifinal game against Brazil, Meazza was tapped to take a penalty shot. But before he could put the ball in position, his shorts fell down! Apparently, the elastic waistband had been torn earlier in the game; now, in front of thousands of spectators, it had finally given way.

Meazza didn't seem fazed by the embarrassing situation, however. He simply hiked up his drawers, set the ball on the ground, and then calmly booted a shot past the astonished goalkeeper.

Fortunately for Italian fans, Meazza's uniform

stayed put throughout the finals. He assisted on two more goals, one by Silvio Piola, the other by Colaussi again, to give his team a 3–1 lead before the half.

The win wasn't in Italy's pocket yet. After the half, Hungary drew within one on a goal by György Sárosi. But as the final ten minutes ticked down, Piola made his second goal of the game to give Italy four on their side of the scoreboard.

Try as they might, the Hungarian players just couldn't make up the difference. When the whistle blew to end the game, the Italians had successfully defended their title as champions of the world!

The Hungarians were, no doubt, disappointed to have come in second. But at least one player tried to see the bigger picture. Referring to Mussolini's "win or die" message, goalkeeper Antal Szabo reportedly quipped, "We may have lost the match, but we saved eleven lives."

What Szabo didn't know—what no one knew—was that all too soon, many, many more than eleven lives would be lost. Within a year, the political tensions that had been simmering throughout Europe began to boil; by 1939, they had erupted into the most catastrophic conflict the world had ever known: World War II.

The Second World War raged throughout Europe, Asia, and Africa for the next six years. Tens of millions of lives were lost and countless cities and towns destroyed. After the war finally ended, it took these nations many long years to recover.

The sporting world suffered losses, too. Athletes from all corners of the globe had joined the fight; thousands never returned from the battlefronts. Those who did survive returned crippled, physically and mentally, or too far past their prime to ever participate in their sport again. Highly anticipated international events, such as the 1940 and 1944 Olympic Games, were canceled. So, too, were the 1942 and 1946 World Cup tournaments.

In fact, it would be twelve years before the World Cup was played again.

CHAPTER FOUR

★ 1950 ★

THE MIRACLE AND THE DEFEAT

The Second World War officially ended on September 2, 1945. Less than a year later, FIFA held its twenty-fifth congress in Luxembourg. Several decisions were made at the meeting, including changing the name of the World Cup trophy to the Jules Rimet Cup, selecting Brazil as the host of the next tournament, and declaring Spanish the official language of the organization. But the most newsworthy accomplishment was the readmittance of the four nations of the British Isles.

At the time, England, Scotland, Ireland, and Wales had some of the biggest and best soccer programs in the world. But they had not been part of FIFA for nearly twenty years because of disagreements concerning the use of amateur players. In 1946, those disagreements were finally resolved, thanks in large part to negotiations by Rimet. To seal the deal, the English team faced off against a team made up of eleven FIFA players in 1947. England won the so-called Match of the Century, 6–1, proof positive that it was one of the top-notch teams around.

But England wasn't the only powerhouse. Thirty-four nations submitted entries for the preliminary rounds of the next World Cup competition, set for 1950. Of the fourteen teams that qualified for the sixteen slots—the other two slots were automatically filled by Brazil, the host country, and Italy, the defending champion—only eleven wound up participating in the Cup. India, Scotland, and Turkey had chosen to withdraw, and although invitations were extended to France and Portugal, neither accepted.

With an uneven field of thirteen teams, the 1950 World Cup followed an unusual format. The teams were divided into four pools, two with four teams each, one with three, and one with just two. The surviving team from each pool would then play in a round-robin final.

Because of its long soccer history and the obvious skill of its players, England was judged as a top contender. But host nation Brazil was high on the list as well and was by far the favorite among soccer-crazy South Americans. Even before competition began, many were predicting that one of these two countries would reign victorious.

Those predictions would not come true, however. In fact, England wouldn't even make it into the final round! The defeat of the English team was even more shocking because it was handed to them, in part, by a very unlikely source: the United States.

Soccer was still a very low-priority sport in the United States in 1950. The US national team was talented but mostly unsupported by the public. Few people even knew there was such a team, let alone cared about its chances to win a competition taking place in a distant country.

But the players themselves cared. Despite clearly being the underdogs of the tournament, they set out to play their hardest. If they were defeated, as everyone assumed they would be, they would at least know they had given it everything they had.

True to expectations, the US team lost its first match to Spain, 3–1. Four days later, the Americans faced England—and delivered one of the greatest upsets the World Cup had, or has, ever known.

On one side of the pitch were the English players, dedicated and highly paid professional athletes who were insured against injury to the tune of three million dollars. On the other were the Americans, a motley crew of amateurs who worked regular jobs for their daily pay.

One of those players was Joseph Gaetjens. Gaetjens was born in Haiti but moved to New York to attend Columbia University. He got a job as a dishwasher in a Brooklyn restaurant to pay his bills. In his free time, he played for one of the city's soccer teams, Brookhattan, where he came to the attention of the US national team's coach in 1949. (Although Gaetjens wasn't a US citizen, he was allowed to join the team just by expressing interest in becoming one.)

The match between England and the United States took place on June 29 before a crowd of ten thousand spectators. The English began their attack right away, dodging around the US defense and firing off shot after shot on Frank Borghi, the US goalkeeper. But to their surprise and dismay, Borghi fended off their attempts. The one shot that looked to be an easy goal instead clanged off the post.

That missed opportunity gave the Americans a much-needed confidence boost. After several minutes of lackluster play, they suddenly came to life. Then, at the thirty-seven-minute mark, midfielder Walter Bahr kicked the ball from twenty-five yards out.

What happened next has gone down in soccer history.

Bert Williams, the English goalkeeper, moved to make the save. At the same time, Gaetjens flew across the field. He dove at the ball and met it with his head. That hit sent the ball on a completely different trajectory—namely, away from Williams and into the net!

The English players were stunned. The *United States* had scored against *them*? Impossible! And what was even more impossible was the fact that England didn't answer that goal with any of its own! Final score: United States 1, England 0.

That's the headline British citizens were greeted with the next morning. Most figured the score had been a typo; the *real* score had to have been England *10*, United States 1. Imagine their shock when they learned the truth!

But their shock was nothing compared to that of many Brazilians two weeks later.

The host country had mounted a strong campaign in the first round to advance to the finals. On the way,

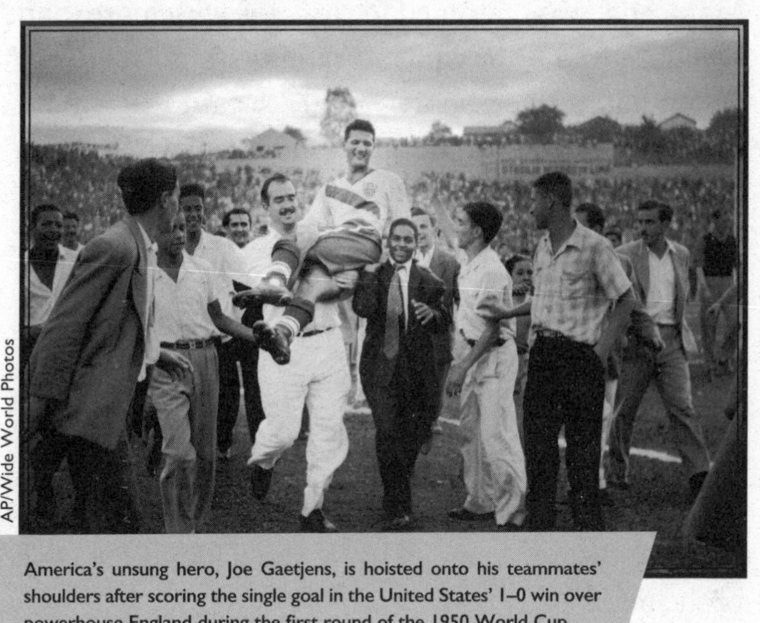
AP/Wide World Photos

America's unsung hero, Joe Gaetjens, is hoisted onto his teammates' shoulders after scoring the single goal in the United States' 1–0 win over powerhouse England during the first round of the 1950 World Cup.

they annihilated Sweden, 7–1, and then dispatched Spain, 6–1. Because of the way the World Cup was scored—a win earned a team two points, a draw one, and a loss zero—Brazil entered its final match, against Uruguay, needing only a draw to take the championship.

The game between Brazil and Uruguay was scheduled for three o'clock on July 16. The stadium,

Maracana, was crammed to capacity, with more than two hundred thousand screaming fans, many of whom had arrived hours earlier, certain they would soon be celebrating their nation's victory over Uruguay. One newspaper echoed that confidence and preprinted its morning edition announcing Brazil as the new World Cup champion.

Needing just a draw, Brazil could easily have played a purely defensive game. But that wasn't how the players wanted to win, so instead they peppered the Uruguayan goalkeeper with multiple shots in the first half. To their surprise, and the crowd's growing dismay, none of those shots found the back of the net.

It wasn't until two minutes into the second half that the spectators got what they wanted.

"Zizinho passed to me," forward Albino Friaça Cardoso recalled years later, referring to his teammate Thomaz Soares da Silva, a.k.a. Zizinho, "and I went past their right winger and their center half. I came into their box, and I shot."

Goal!

The fans erupted with joyful cheers. Confetti and ribbons rained down on the field. Gunpowder explosions sent clouds of smoke billowing over the stands.

But, as one Brazilian later observed, "We forgot something very important. This Uruguayan team was excellent. And our team wasn't as excellent as we thought."

One Uruguayan player suddenly started to cause trouble for the Brazilians. Right winger Alcides Ghiggia was an excellent dribbler and playmaker. At the sixty-six-minute mark, he put both skills to use. He dribbled the ball around a defender who slipped trying to stop him. Then he crossed the touchline and sent the ball to his teammate Juan Schiaffino. Schiaffino turned, aimed, and shot. The ball soared past Brazil's keeper, Moacir Barbosa Nascimento, and swished against the net strings.

The Brazilians had hoped to go out with a win, but a draw was fine, too, since it would still give them the championship. All they had to do was prevent Uruguay from scoring another goal in the next twenty-four minutes.

They didn't. With eleven minutes remaining, Ghiggia struck again.

A short, grainy, black-and-white film clip, eerily

silent, captured the historic moment. Ghiggia collected the ball on the right wing, saw the defense out of position, and kicked. The ball rose a foot off the ground and curled toward the net. Barbosa, alone in front of the net, couldn't make the save. Goal for Uruguay!

The fans, so raucous just seconds before, fell into a deep, shocked silence—a silence that continued through the rest of the game and for many days afterward throughout the streets of Rio de Janeiro and in the country beyond. After all, no one in Brazil had reason to cheer. Their team, their pride and glory, had been defeated, two goals to one.

CHAPTER FIVE

★ 1954 ★

THE MIGHTY FALL

When FIFA met in 1946 they selected Brazil as the host country for the 1950 World Cup and Switzerland for the 1954 contest. The number of entrants for the second postwar competition grew from thirty-four in 1950 to forty-five in 1954. Unlike the 1950 Cup, which saw only thirteen teams in the tournament, this Cup had all sixteen slots filled, making it easier for FIFA to format the rounds of play. The sixteen teams were split into four groups of four for the first round. Two winners from each group moved on to the quarterfinals; the four teams that then emerged victorious went on to semifinal play, with the top two advancing to the finals.

This year's tournament saw three newcomers to the field, the most notable being Scotland. Scotland, like its neighbor England, had a long and fruitful soccer past. Many expected the nation to do well.

It did not. In its first match it faced Austria (which had been declared an independent country again after World War II, even as Germany was being divided into East and West) and lost, 1–0. Then it was stunned by the defending champion, Uruguay, by a demoralizing seven goals to none.

It may have been small consolation to the Scots when other teams lost by equal or even greater margins. In Group 2, South Korea—making its first World Cup appearance—fell twice, once to Hungary, 9–0, and then to Turkey, 7–0. The Turks discovered how humiliating such a loss could be when, three days later, they were crushed by the West Germans, 7–2. West Germany could have sympathized, however, having lost to Hungary, 8–3, in earlier play!

Scores like these, more typical of baseball games than soccer matches, had fans jumping with excitement and defenders scratching their heads in bewilderment. But the shoot-out wasn't over yet. In the first game of the quarterfinals, Switzerland landed an amazing three goals in the first nineteen minutes of play. Normally, those goals would have given the Swiss an insurmountable lead. But the host country's defense fell apart in the ten minutes before halftime, giving up five goals to Austria! The Austrians took the game, 7–5—a tournament record number of goals in one game.

The other quarterfinal matches weren't quite as high scoring. When the dust had settled, Austria was joined by West Germany, Hungary, and Uruguay in the semifinals. Left behind with Switzerland were England, Brazil, and Yugoslavia. This last team had surprised many by beating out France and tying Brazil earlier in the tournament.

Of the final four teams, the Hungarians were considered the best. They were the gold-medal champs of the 1952 Summer Olympics, had a four-year record of twenty-three wins and four draws, and had recently beaten England at Wembley Stadium—the first time any visiting team had ever defeated the English on their home soil. It came as no surprise to anyone, therefore, that Hungary advanced to the semifinals by beating Brazil and then to the finals, where it faced West Germany.

The Germans ran onto the pitch burning to reverse their humiliating 8–3 loss to Hungary. But at least one Hungarian player was equally eager for revenge. Team captain Ferenc Puskás had been hacked by Germany's center half in their earlier meeting. He'd sat out the quarterfinal and semifinal games, nursing an injured ankle. When the Hungarians won their way to the finals without him, he was delighted—and determined to join the team on the field regardless of the pain.

The Germans were delighted to have him in the opposing lineup. A formidable foe when healthy, the limping Puskás would no doubt do more harm than good for the Hungarians.

But as it turned out, all the players would have trouble with their footing in that final game. Rain had started before the game and continued throughout, turning the pitch into a slippery, muddy mess that found more than one player landing face-first in the slop.

If Puskás was bothered by the mud or his ankle injury, he didn't show it. Instead, he attacked the Germans' goal and, in the sixth minute, scored! Less than two minutes later, the Hungarians added a second goal when Germany's keeper bobbled the ball right in front of Zoltán Czibor. All the forward from Hungary had to do was knock it into the net, which he did.

The Germans didn't give up, however. They chalked up two of their own to tie the game, 2–2, at the break.

Defense took center stage in the second half of the game, with neither team able to break the tie. Then, as the clock clicked into the eighty-fourth minute of the match, Germany's right forward, Helmut Rahn, raced in, claimed the ball with his left foot, and kicked.

Thump! The shot sailed into the far corner of the goal! The West Germans had the lead!

Puskás made one final, desperate attempt to level the score. He might have succeeded, too, but for one small problem: the referee whistled him offside when he made his shot. Although the ball swished into the net, it was discounted. Minutes later, the game ended. The Germans had beaten the seemingly unbeatable Hungarians, 3–2.

As was traditional, aging FIFA president Jules Rimet presented the Cup to the winning coach. It was a bittersweet moment for Rimet. After thirty-three years as FIFA's leader, he was retiring from the organization. Handing over the Cup was his last official act.

Rimet died just two years later. Thanks to his efforts, soccer and the World Cup had gained worldwide recognition. Sadly, however, he passed away without ever meeting the player who would singlehandedly catapult international soccer into the sports stratosphere.

CHAPTER SIX

★ 1958 ★

WHAT'S IN A NAME?

Edson Arantes do Nascimento doesn't know how he got his nickname. He doesn't know what it means, either. But he does know he didn't like it at first. He got used to hearing it over time, however—lucky, considering it was the name hundreds of thousands of people screamed for decades during soccer games. In fact, ask most people to name one soccer player, and it's the name they'll give you:

"PELÉ!"

Pelé was born on October 23, 1940, in a small town in Brazil. He grew up poor, with no money for soccer equipment. That didn't stop him from playing his favorite game, though. He and his friends made balls out of old socks stuffed with newspapers. They formed teams and played barefoot on dusty dirt roads. His happiest days were the ones when he played soccer from sunup to sundown.

Even as a youngster, Pelé was remarkably talented. He was just fifteen years old when a famous soccer player named Waldemar de Brito discovered him. De Brito helped Pelé get on a professional team called Santos, named after the team's hometown.

Pelé played for Santos from 1956 until 1974. He also played on Brazil's national team during those years. It was as a member of that squad that he first caught the attention of the world.

Pelé was seventeen years old when he traveled to Sweden for the 1958 World Cup. As in 1954, all sixteen slots were filled, allowing for the same format of four pools of four teams for the initial rounds of play. Brazil was grouped with Austria, England, and the Soviet Union.

The Soviets were making their first appearance in the Cup. They beat out England to advance to the quarterfinals. England's loss didn't come as a surprise, but it did sadden many soccer fans. On February 6, 1958, the English team had suffered a tragedy when a plane carrying forty-four people crashed. Twenty-three passengers perished, eight of whom were English soccer players. The team simply couldn't recover, emotionally or practically, after such a tremendous loss.

The Soviet Union didn't move beyond the quarterfinals, however, being beaten by Sweden. Brazil stayed alive with a 1–0 victory over Wales, which was also in the World Cup for the first time. France and defending champion West Germany also reached the semifinal round.

On June 24, the Germans battled the Swedes in an exciting match that was tied at the half. But Germany couldn't survive the host nation's onslaught. They allowed two goals in the remaining forty-five minutes while failing to put one in their opponents' net. Sweden was through to the finals.

Meanwhile, on that same day in the city of Solna, twenty-seven thousand fans witnessed the emergence of soccer's superstar.

Brazil had drawn France as its opponent in the semifinal round. With two high-scoring games under their belts in the tournament, the French players hit the field full of confidence. Brazil quickly deflated them, however, with a goal a mere two minutes into play. But France answered soon after to tie things up. Then Brazil's star player, Didi (born Valdir Pereira), blasted one into the net at the thirty-nine-minute mark.

A one-goal lead is nice, but not impossible to overcome. No one knew that better than Brazil's youngest player. Pelé had watched his team from the sidelines in earlier games, nursing a knee injury. Fortunately, he was back on the field in time to play against the

Soviets in the third game. He had played well that match, working in tandem with another of the team's stars, Manuel "Garrincha" dos Santos, but he hadn't been a standout. People started to sit up and take notice of him in the quarterfinal against Wales, however, when he scored the game's single goal.

But it was in the second half of the semifinal against France that he truly stormed the scene. Within twenty-three minutes he scored not one, not two, but *three* goals! He was the youngest player in World Cup history to earn a hat trick. France simply couldn't stop him. The final score was Brazil 5, France 2.

Sweden and Brazil met on June 29. More than fifty thousand fans crowded into the stadium in Solna. Countless others watched from the comfort of their homes, for the World Cup was being televised internationally for the first time ever. Black-and-white film footage of the game, which still exists, captured each goal as well as the reactions of the players and the spectators.

The Swedes drew first blood with a slashing shot by Nils Liedholm just four minutes into the game. The score didn't stay at 1–0 for long. Less than five minutes later Garrincha snared the ball, flew down the right sideline, cut toward the goal, and threaded a pass through the defense to his teammate Edvaldo Izídio Neto, or Vavá, as he was known. Vavá sent the ball right into the net to tie the game at one apiece.

It was Garrincha to Vavá again twenty-three minutes later with an almost identical play, resulting in Brazil's second goal. The first half ended with the score still at Brazil 2, Sweden 1.

That's where it stayed through the first ten minutes of the second half. Then, with the clock showing fifty-five, Pelé received a high pass in front of the goal. As defenders swarmed to cover him, he bounced the ball once on his thigh and then sent it arcing over the closest Swede. As the Swedish player's momentum carried him forward, Pelé dodged around, retrieved the ball, and powered it with a mighty kick into the goal.

It was an amazing point that brought fans leaping to their feet and Pelé jumping for joy into the arms of his teammates. Three to one, Brazil. Thirteen minutes later, it was 4–1, Brazil, thanks to a low-dribbling kick by Mario Zagallo.

Agne Simonsson of Sweden tightened the gap soon after by drawing out Brazilian goalkeeper Gilmar and boosting a shot on the unprotected goal. Now there were only ten minutes remaining in the game. If the Swedes were going to tie or overcome their two-point deficit, they would have to move quickly and decisively.

They didn't. Instead, it was Pelé who made the move. In the final moments of World Cup 1958, the seventeen-year-old raced to meet a lobbing pass in front of the goal. The Swedish keeper, Karl Svensson, ran to the same spot, as did two of his teammates. Pelé and one defender reached the ball at nearly the same time. They jumped, heads cocked to intercept the ball.

Pelé got there first. With a solid header, he punched the ball up and over Svensson's reaching arms. The ball took one big hop and then gently bounced into the net. Goal number two for Pelé—and Brazil's first World Cup victory!

Pelé broke down in tears of joy. His teammates boosted him on their shoulders, supporting him as he sagged from sheer exhaustion and overwhelming happiness. The fans, while disappointed that their home team hadn't won, still cheered heartily as the victors grabbed edges of Brazil's flag and ran with it around the pitch. They cheered even louder when the Brazilians honored the host country by exchanging their flag for the Swedish one and running another lap.

And when those fans left the stadium hours later, there was one name on everyone's lips. The name had no real meaning in any language. But for those who spoke the language of soccer, that name soon became synonymous with greatness: Pelé.

CHAPTER SEVEN

★ 1962 ★

TWICE IS NICE

In the years following his World Cup debut, Pelé continued to amaze crowds with his athleticism, instincts, and winning personality. Soccer fans everywhere couldn't wait to see what he would do when he took to the field for the 1962 tournament in Chile.

They were not disappointed in his performance in Brazil's opening match against Mexico. That game, Pelé scored his team's second goal in the 2–0 victory.

Unfortunately, that was his only point in the tournament. In fact, it was his only full game. Three days later, Brazil faced Czechoslovakia. Early in the match, Pelé suddenly fell, clutching his left thigh. He had torn a muscle and was out for the rest of the Cup.

On that same day, June 2, one of the most vicious soccer games in World Cup history was played. Dubbed the "Battle of Santiago" for the city in which it was held, the match saw players from Chile and Italy coming to blows on the field.

The tension between the two teams had been brewing for weeks. In their newspapers, Italy had branded Chile a country of illiterate alcoholics. Then Chile had accused Italy of stealing its best players. Animosity grew to a fever pitch, and when the day of the game arrived, the Chilean fans were crying for blood. The Italian players tried to defuse the situation by throwing roses to the crowd. Their offerings were met with jeers and taunts. And soon after, things went from bad to worse.

From the starting whistle on, players kicked, shoved, and spat at one another. Within minutes, one of Italy's players, Giorgio Ferrini, was ejected for rough tackling. Not long afterward, Chile's Leonel Sánchez threw Humberto Maschio, a native of Argentina, to the ground and punched him in the nose. Sánchez was the son of a boxer and clearly knew how to hit—Maschio's nose was broken.

Amazingly, Sánchez wasn't tossed from the game. But being on the field made him a prime target. A short time later, Mario David avenged his teammate's broken nose with a slashing high kick at

Sánchez's throat. The referee blew his whistle; David was ejected.

With the Italian team down two of their starting players, the Chilean squad was able to post two goals in the second half for a 2–0 win. Later, officials said they would have stopped the game to allow players time to cool off but feared that doing so would have caused a riot. "The most stupid, appalling, disgusting, and disgraceful exhibition of football," the British Broadcasting Company called the game.

Meanwhile, other teams were mounting attacks against one another, although they saved their kicks for the ball, not their opponents. But in the semifinal match between Brazil and Chile, blows were exchanged yet again. This time, it was Brazil's star player, Garrincha, whose fists flew in fury.

As a child, Garrincha had suffered a bout of polio, a disease that often leaves victims crippled for life. Garrincha had recovered, but the polio had left him with oddly misshapen legs. Those legs never slowed him down, however. He was one of the sport's best ball handlers and playmakers, a jokester whose humor often relieved his teammates' stress before games.

But Garrincha wasn't laughing when, fed up by the rough handling he was receiving from a Chilean rival, he threw a punch. A fight broke out that ended only when Garrincha was ordered from the field. He left amid a shower of debris from riled-up spectators. Not that his departure changed the outcome of the game; Brazil won, 4–2, to advance to the finals.

The next day, debate swirled over whether Garrincha would be allowed to play in the final match against Czechoslovakia. Fortunately for his teammates and the Brazilian fans, he was. The South American squad would need every good player it had if it was to be successful against the Czechoslovakians.

Czechoslovakia had clawed its way to the finals with a 1–0 win over Hungary in the quarterfinals and a 3–1 victory against Yugoslavia in the semis. Josef Masopust was their top scorer, but the backbone of their team was their goalkeeper, Vilem Schroif. Schroif had been remarkably effective in the games leading up to the finals. He looked to shut down Brazil's attack.

But Schroif might as well have tried to hold back a flood with a teaspoon. Even without Pelé, the Brazilian offense was packed with talent. While the Czechs surprised everyone by getting on the board first with a sixteenth-minute point by Masopust, the Brazilians powered back with a shot from Pelé's replacement, Amarildo Tavares da Silveira, that squeaked between Schroif and the post to swish into the net.

Amarildo helped his team to their second goal, too, with a blistering pass across the field to teammate José Ely "Zito" de Miranda, who headed the ball into the net. Brazil now had the lead, 2–1.

The late-afternoon sun may have played a part in Brazil's third and final goal. Defender Djalma Santos lobbed a kick in the air toward the goal. It should have been a routine catch for Schroif, but the sun's glare may have blinded him for just a second—long enough for him to lose track of the ball. He bobbled the catch right in front of Vavá, who simply knocked it in for goal number three.

Czechoslovakia couldn't recover. When the game ended twelve minutes later, Brazil had won its second consecutive World Cup!

CHAPTER EIGHT

★ 1966 ★

NO THREE-PEAT

In 1966, the World Cup was hosted by soccer's birthplace, England. The country was home to hundreds of thousands of rabid fans who wanted what had so far eluded them in their World Cup appearances: the Jules Rimet Cup.

As was customary, the gold trophy made its way to the host country months before the tournament began. Rather than keeping it under lock and key, the English handlers chose to display it in a London shop window along with a collection of rare stamps. Imagine their horror when one morning they found the window empty!

A frantic search for the iconic Cup turned up nothing at first. In fact, the trophy might never have been found if not for the sharp nose of a little black-and-white dog named Pickles. Pickles and his owner were out for a walk when suddenly the dog started digging at a hedge. When the owner inspected the site, he discovered the trophy, wrapped in newspaper.

He returned it to the proper officials, who no doubt handled it more carefully after that!

In the days leading up to the first match, speculation centered on Brazil's chances of being the first country to "three-peat." Many believed that with Pelé back in the lineup, along with Garrincha and other players from the previous two victories, the defending champions looked good to take the Cup again.

But it was not to be. Targeted from the outset by vicious tackles, the Brazilians were literally knocked out of contention in the first round. Pelé, in particular, had been hacked repeatedly on the field. He was so badly hurt, in fact, that he couldn't play in the second match, which Brazil lost, 3–1, to Hungary.

He was back on the field for game three against Portugal, but as film shows, he again took hit after hit. He left the game, a 3–1 loss, limping and bruised. Disappointed and furious at the brutality, Pelé declared that he would never compete in another World Cup.

"Soccer has been distorted by violence and destructive tactics," he told reporters. "I don't want to end up an invalid."

With Pelé and Brazil out of the picture, all eyes turned to the play of an amazing newcomer from Portugal, twenty-four-year-old Eusébio da Silva Ferreira.

His skillful dribbling, combined with his uncanny ability to find the open shot, made him an instant star in soccer-crazed England. With Eusébio leading the charge, the Portuguese reached the quarterfinals.

Portugal's opponent in this round was North Korea. The fact that the North Koreans had made it so far in the tournament came as a surprise to many. They were only in the World Cup because several other nations had dropped out after qualifying. Once in, however, they fought hard to stay in. After falling to the Soviet Union, they tied Chile and then, unbelievably, ousted Italy, 1–0.

The North Koreans looked incredibly strong at the start of their quarterfinal match. In just twenty-five minutes of play, they scored three times!

But then Eusébio took over. Two minutes after North Korea's third point, he boosted the ball into the goal. Two minutes before the break, he hit another. After the half, he made back-to-back penalty kicks—and assisted his teammate José Augusto for the team's fifth goal!

It was goodbye, North Korea; hello, semifinals for the Portuguese. That was as far as they went, however. Try as they might, they couldn't overcome the onslaught by their English opponents. The star of the show that game was Bobby Charlton, who sent the home fans into a frenzy by scoring both of his team's goals. Eusébio was held to just one, a penalty kick in the final minutes.

While Portugal was falling to England, the Soviet Union was collapsing beneath the powerful play of West Germany. The 1966 World Cup finals would be between the English and the Germans.

The match was played before a sellout crowd at Wembley Stadium in London. The fans buzzed with excitement in the opening minutes—only to fall silent at the twelve-minute mark as Helmut Haller of Germany turned a pass at the right corner of the box into the game's first goal.

Geoff Hurst tied it up soon afterward when he headed a free kick over and past Germany's goalkeeper. The score stayed knotted for the remainder of the first half and far into the second as well. Then, with just thirteen minutes left to play, Martin Peters of England captured the ball near the front of the goal's mouth and converted it into a point with a smashing kick.

The fans went wild. Their screams of joy and encouragement grew louder and louder as the final minutes ticked down. England, birthplace of soccer, was going to win its first World Cup!

Or was it?

Moments before the referee blew his whistle to signal the end of the game, Germany's Wolfgang Weber chased down a loose ball that had rolled free near England's goal. With one swift and decisive blast, he sent it to the back of the net! The score was tied—and the game was forced into extra time.

Those final minutes would yield one of the most controversial plays in World Cup history. Nearly ten minutes in, Hurst snared a cross pass from Alan Ball in front of the German goal. He turned and booted a hard shot. The ball flew through the air, struck the goal's crossbar, and slammed straight down to a point just inside the line.

Goal! The fans and players went insane until—*fweet!* The linesman blew his whistle and rushed forward, arms waving. From his point of view, the ball hadn't struck *behind* the line, but in *front* of it! There was no goal!

The linesman and the referee met on the pitch. As they conferred, soccer fans the world over held their breath. Goal or no goal?

They got their answer a second later. The officials ruled that the ball had, indeed, hit inside the line. The goal was good! The English were ahead

3–2! And before the extra minutes ended, they were ahead 4–2, thanks to yet *another* goal by the jubilant Hurst. His hat trick was the first, and so far only, ever made during a Men's World Cup championship game—and with it, he delivered England's first, and so far only, World Cup victory.

CHAPTER NINE

★ 1970 ★

THE RETURN OF THE KING

Pelé was back. After vowing never to play in another World Cup, he had decided to return after all. Key to his decision was a new rule enacted by FIFA.

To address the rough tackling that overshadowed the 1966 World Cup, FIFA established a card system that gave referees the power to first warn, and then eject, any player they caught purposefully attacking an opponent. A yellow card was a warning; a red card was an expulsion.

Amazingly, Pelé's decision to play was almost nullified by Brazil's coach, João Saldanha, who, for some inexplicable reason, cut Pelé from the team! The public outcry against this move was instantaneous—and very, very angry. Pelé was reinstated almost as quickly as Saldanha was replaced. The team's new coach, Mario Zagallo, proved his worth by building one of the best offenses in soccer history. Spearheading that offense was Pelé, the man once declared a national treasure by the Brazilian government.

Brazil coasted through the preliminaries, winning all of its six qualifying matches. The team was equally successful in the first round of group play, going undefeated against Czechoslovakia, Romania, and the defending champion, England. The game against the English was won by a single goal—although it probably would have been a two-goal victory if not for Gordon Banks.

Banks was England's goalkeeper. In the 1966 World Cup, he had prevented teams from Mexico, France, Argentina, and Portugal from scoring a single goal. Only West Germany, in the finals, had managed to get two past him.

He added another goalless game in England's first match of the 1970 Cup by denying Romania. Next up was Brazil.

The Brazilians were fully aware of Banks's abilities. That knowledge may have helped them do what so few others had done: namely, get one past him. The goal was made by Jairzinho, one of Brazil's top players, in the fifty-ninth minute. But it was the goal that *wasn't* made earlier in the game that had fans all over the world cheering.

Brazil was on the attack, rocketing down the field toward Banks. The ball nearly rolled out of bounds but was captured by Jairzinho. He hooked a pass across to the net to Pelé, who was covered by an English defender. Both jumped to intercept. Pelé jumped higher and met the ball with his head.

Banks, meanwhile, leaped into the air, anticipating that the ball would fly high. Instead, the ball shot toward the lower right corner of the net. There was no way Banks should have been able to save it. But he did, somehow twisting his body in midair and stretching just far enough to swat the ball away before it crossed into the net.

"He came from nowhere," a dumbfounded Pelé recalled later. "I was already shouting 'Gooooal!' "

"My first reaction was to look at Pelé," Banks remembered. "He'd ground to a halt. That's all I needed to know."

Behind such stellar play, both Brazil and England made it to the quarterfinals. But that was the end of the road for England, who fell to West Germany in overtime play. The Germans didn't make it further than the semifinals, however. They were beaten four goals to three in extra minutes by Italy.

That Italy had netted four goals was something of a surprise: the team was known for its defense, not its offense. They would need every defensive trick in the book if they were to win against Brazil, their opponent in the finals.

Pelé drove the frontline force. He scored early in the game with a header off a pass from Roberto Rivelino that caught the Italian goalkeeper napping. Not surprisingly, the Italian team covered the Brazilian superstar with extra care after that, and at the same time they managed to post a goal of their own.

The score was tied at the half, but then the Italians' energy began to flag. Perhaps Mexico's heat or the thin air of the high elevation was getting to them. Or maybe they were simply exhausted from the Brazilians' continuous push.

Whatever the cause, they weren't playing their best in the second half. The Brazilians, on the other hand, were on fire. First Gérson de Oliveira Nunes hit, to put Brazil up, 2–1. Then Pelé tricked the Italian goalkeeper with a fake header that turned into a pass to Jairzinho, who converted it into the team's third goal. It was Pelé again with a perfectly aimed pass to team captain Carlos Alberto, who thundered the ball into the net for goal number four.

That shot, ranked among the best ever taken in World Cup history, was the nail in Italy's coffin. When the final seconds ticked away, Brazil had its third World Cup victory! The win had been so decisive that not even the Italian media could find fault. "The best footballers in the world" was what they called the players from South America.

Of those "best footballers," Pelé was the cream of the crop. He was undeniably the most recognizable soccer player in the world, and his jaw-dropping play was matched only by his friendly demeanor on and off the field. Take his reaction to the Gordon Banks save: rather than storming away in frustration as another player might have, Pelé congratulated the goalkeeper with a pat on the back. That same game also saw him exchange jerseys, hugs, and smiles with England's Bobby Moore, a moment caught in a now-famous photograph. Always willing to sign autographs, Pelé was and continues to be the sport's most congenial goodwill ambassador.

But those hoping to catch a glimpse of the superstar in the next World Cup were to be disappointed. The 1970 competition was Pelé's last, although he continued to play for Brazil's Santos team until his retirement in 1974. He relaced his cleats less than a year later, but for a different team and on a different continent. In 1975, he became a member of the New York Cosmos. He played for them until his final game in October of 1977.

Pelé's influence on the world of soccer was singular, but his ability to reach out to his rivals left an even bigger mark. As the Brazilian ambassador to the United Nations once said, "Pelé played football for twenty-two years, and in that time he did more to promote world friendship and fraternity than any other ambassador anywhere."

A British newspaper described him somewhat differently: "How do you spell Pelé? G-O-D."

AP/Wide World Photos

Pelé heads in a goal over his Italian rival, to put Brazil up 1–0 in the 1970 World Cup final.

CHAPTER TEN

★ 1974 ★

TOTAL FOOTBALL

The 1974 World Cup competition, held in West Germany, bid goodbye to longtime favorites England and Hungary while welcoming four newcomers: Australia, Haiti, Zaire, and East Germany. It also welcomed a new format for the final stages of play. Rather than single knockout quarterfinals, the eight top teams were separated into two groups, A and B. The four teams within each group played one another, a total of three games apiece, with the best team then advancing on to the final.

The 1974 tournament saw other changes as well. A new solid-gold trophy, called simply the World Cup Trophy, replaced the Jules Rimet Trophy, which had been retired by Brazil after its victory in the previous Cup. Taking the helm of FIFA was João Havelange, the first non-European to become president. Also noteworthy was the first red card, given to Chilean player Carlos Caszely for excessive roughness.

But by far the most exciting new development was a style of play known as "Total Football."

For years, soccer teams were made up of players who were assigned set positions on the forward line, the midfield, the defensive zone, or the goal. While they could stray from their slots on occasion, mostly they were expected to stay put and cover their territory.

Total Football turned that concept on its head. Now, instead of being pigeonholed in their roles, teammates moved freely among the positions, adapting their play to whatever action unfolded on the field. No position was left uncovered; if a midfielder raced toward the opponent's goal with the ball, for example, his teammates quickly shifted about until his empty position was filled.

Total Football required players to know how to play every position and how to "read" the field. It demanded that they be flexible, ready to move fluidly into a different spot on the field at a second's notice. In 1974, no player was better at that than Johan Cruyff of the Netherlands.

Cruyff was slim, nimble-footed, and the only soccer player to have a move named after him. The "Cruyff turn," as it is known, is a trick aimed at luring a defender one step out of position. To do the move, the handler controls the ball with his right foot and pretends to move right. When the defender moves with him, the handler then flicks the ball *behind* his own feet—and away from the defender. After that, it's a simple matter of controlling the ball and heading straight for the goal.

Considered one of the sport's top playmakers, Cruyff captured the attention of the world during the 1974 World Cup with his uncanny ability to be in the right place at the right time. Behind his wily expertise and pinpoint accuracy, the Netherlands reached the finals for the first time ever.

There they faced the home team, West Germany, in its first appearance in the finals since its 1966 loss to England. The Germans had won all but one of their opening matches. They lost a politically charged match with East Germany in which the only and winning goal was scored by Jürgen Sparwasser. Still, the West Germans advanced to the second stage of play. There, Yugoslavia and Sweden fell to them by scores of 2–0 and 4–2.

Their third game in this pool was against Poland—and it might as well have taken place *in* a pool, for the pitch was a rain-soaked mess of mud that slowed both sides to a crawl. Neither team scored in the first half; it wasn't until the seventy-sixth minute that the ball found the back of the net. That goal, made by Germany's Gerd Müller, was the only one of the game. Poland was left to battle Brazil for third place, while the West Germans moved on to the finals against the Netherlands.

The final match took place in the Olympiastadion in Munich on July 7. Security at the game—throughout the tournament, in fact—was tighter than it ever had been before, and with good reason.

Two years earlier, Munich had hosted the Summer Olympics. Midway through the competition, a horrifying event took place. Eight Palestinian terrorists took eleven Israeli athletes hostage. They killed two of the hostages and attempted to use the other nine as human shields when they fled the country via airplane. At the airport, the Munich police's rescue efforts went terribly wrong. All the hostages, as well as three terrorists, were killed.

Now, two years later, no one was taking any chances. Security forces, including tanks, were present at airports, and each venue was guarded carefully. Fortunately, the terrible events of 1972 were not repeated at the World Cup.

The battle for the new World Cup Trophy began

at four o'clock. Amazingly, one minute after four, the Netherlands scored their first goal! Even more amazingly, West Germany hadn't even touched the ball!

The point came from a penalty kick awarded to the Dutch when Cruyff, dribbling toward the goal, was tackled by Uli Hoeness inside the box. What followed was another World Cup first—the first penalty kick to be taken in a finals match. Johan Neeskens took the kick, calmly booting the ball past goalkeeper Sepp Maier.

Then something curious happened. The Dutch coach Rinus Michels, the man who had developed Total Football for his players, decided to fall back on defense rather than allow his team to put their tried-and-true strategy to work. His decision was based on a desire to protect their one-point lead.

But it backfired. An overzealous sliding tackle by the Netherlands' Wim Jansen gave the West Germans a penalty kick of their own. Paul Breitner lined up his shot and trotted forward. Jan Jongbloed, the Dutch goalkeeper, thought Breitner was aiming toward the right side, and so took a side step in that direction. Instead, the kick sent the ball flying toward the lower left corner. Jongbloed was too far out of position to block it.

Tie score, 1–1.

In the minutes remaining in the first half, the two teams fought hard to unravel the knot. Berti Vogts of Germany nearly booted one past Jongbloed, but Jongbloed made the save. Later, Cruyff dished the ball off to teammate Jonny Rep. Rep nearly converted the pass into a goal, but was robbed when Maier stopped the ball.

It wasn't until the forty-third minute that the score changed. Germany's Rainer Bonhof had the ball. He dribbled madly down the right sideline and then angled in toward the goal. He darted around a defender and launched a pass to Müller, who had raced to the front of the goal.

But Müller bobbled the ball! It bounced a few feet behind him. With lightning-quick reflexes, he darted around and snared the loose ball. Then, with a twisting kick, he fired the ball toward the goal—and past Jongbloed!

It was Müller's fourteenth goal of the World Cup, a record at the time. He and his teammates leaped and celebrated on the field. In the stands, the fans went wild. And when neither team scored in the second half, they went even crazier. Twenty years after winning the 1954 World Cup, the West Germans were the champions once more!

Cruyff and his teammates naturally were upset with their performance. "Germany didn't win. We lost it," Cruyff told reporters. Cruyff himself had done all he could, in that game as well as in the preceding matches. In fact, he had a hand—or rather, a foot—in all of the Netherlands' nineteen World Cup goals.

But in the end, his individual performance didn't matter to him. The Cup was in Germany's hands.

AP/Wide World Photos

Wily Johan Cruyff of the Netherlands avoids Argentina's goalkeeper to score a goal in the 1974 World Cup.

CHAPTER ELEVEN

★ 1978 ★

WORKING THE SYSTEM?

In 1966, FIFA awarded the host duties for the 1978 World Cup to Argentina. The government immediately went into a frenzy of planning, building, and beautifying their country in anticipation of taking center stage before the world.

What the country's leaders didn't anticipate, however, was that they would be forced from power two years before the tournament took place. The South American country was still struggling to quell civil unrest and uncertainty as the time for the World Cup tournament approached. In light of this, many national teams petitioned for a change to a safer venue.

The requests were denied. Instead, João Havelange worked with the new Argentine government to ensure that the competition would go as smoothly as possible. Luckily, his efforts paid off.

After many months of preliminary rounds, in which a record number of ninety-five teams competed for the fourteen available slots, the 1978 World Cup kicked off on June 1. All but two of the sixteen teams—Iran and Tunisia—had played in previous tournaments, and three teams, Brazil, West Germany, and Italy, were returning with more than one championship already under their belts. But this year, the team most people were watching had never won a Cup—although it had come very close four years before.

Behind its innovative Total Football strategy, the team from the Netherlands had rocketed through the qualifiers, winning five of its six matches. In the course of those games, the Dutch booted in eleven goals while giving up only three. Many expected them to repeat their previous World Cup efforts and go all the way to the finals.

And that's just what they did, although they didn't get there as easily as some thought they would. After dumping Iran, 3–0, in their first game, they found themselves locked in a tie with the determined and surprisingly strong team from Peru—and then on the wrong side of a 3–2 score in a game against Scotland. Instead of a commanding first-place rank at the end of the first round, the Netherlands wound up in second.

That placing might have been just the wake-up call the Dutch players needed. After their lackluster showing in the openers, they thumped Austria, 5–1;

tied the 1974 West German champs, 2–2; and won a hard-fought battle against Italy, 2–1. Those scores were good enough to see them through to the finals.

Meanwhile, Argentina was busy slicing its way past its opponents to reach its first finals in nearly half a century. On the way there, the team may have received a boost that, while not illegal, had fans from rival Brazil crying foul.

Brazil, Argentina, Poland, and Peru were put together in Group B for the second stage of play. The winner of this stage would advance to the finals. On June 14, Brazil beat Peru, 3–0. Two and a half hours later, Argentina beat Poland, 2–0. Four days later, Poland beat Peru, knocking that nation out of contention. Meanwhile, Brazil and Argentina ended their match in a 0–0 draw.

There were now two games left to go in the round. First up was Brazil against Poland. Brazil won, 3–1, thus assuring them second place in Group B at the very least. If Argentina should lose or tie in its upcoming match with Peru, Brazil would go on to the finals. Even if Argentina won, Brazil had a chance of advancing: if its total goals for the round were greater than Argentina's, Brazil would be declared the round's overall victor.

This is when things got interesting. According to rumors, the Peruvians didn't want the Brazilians to advance. Peru's goalkeeper had a particular reason for wanting Argentina to succeed—he was a native-born Argentine. Some believed he feared that if he prevented Argentina from scoring, then his country of birth would hate him forever.

Whether the rumors were true or not, the results remained the same. The team from Peru gave up two goals in the first half and then four more in the second. Those six unanswered goals were enough to push Argentina into the finals—and leave the Brazilians seething at the injustice of the schedule. After all, if the Peruvians hadn't known the results of the Brazil-Poland match, they wouldn't have known how many goals Argentina needed to win the finals slot. Without that knowledge they might have played harder, perhaps even unseated the Argentines.

But Brazil's protests fell on deaf ears—for the time being, anyway.

The final match between the Netherlands and the host country was scheduled to be played at three o'clock on June 25. A crowd of nearly seventy-two thousand rabid soccer fans filled the stands hours before. As the time drew near, they grew more and more excited. Then, at last, the locker room doors opened and out came the Dutch players resplendent in their electric-orange jerseys.

But where were the Argentine players? Usually, both teams filed onto the field side by side. This year, however, Argentina's coach, César Luis Menotti, had decided to psych out the rival squad. He kept the Dutch waiting on the field for ten minutes; with each minute that ticked by, the Dutch became more and more agitated. They had hit the pitch charged up and ready to play, but now that energy was turning sour!

Menotti's tactic had only a temporary effect on the Dutch players, however. Once the game began, they settled down and found their rhythm. So did the Argentines. The first half saw both launching attack after attack. Both threatened to get on the board first, yet after more than thirty minutes, the game was still scoreless.

Then, in the thirty-eighth minute, hometown hero Mario Kempes took control. Kempes had starred in earlier wins by Argentina, scoring four of his team's eight goals in the second stage of play. Now he thrilled spectators by collecting a pass from Leopoldo Luque and drilling it across the confetti-covered pitch and into the net.

The score remained at Argentina 1, Netherlands 0, throughout the first half. After the break, the Dutch pushed even harder than before, yet time and again failed to get one by the Argentine goalkeeper. It wasn't until eight minutes before the end of the game that they finally managed to tie things up with a spectacular header by Dick Nanninga.

The battle raged on through the final minutes of regulation play with neither team adding to their score. The game would be decided in overtime.

While no game is ever won by a single player, it can be argued that one man made the difference for his team in this final. In the 105th minute, Mario Kempes danced through a sea of defenders toward the goal. Jongbloed charged out and stopped Kempes's kick—only to watch in horror as Kempes darted around him and nudged the ball into the net!

And Kempes wasn't finished. As the 115th minute approached, he found teammate Daniel Bertoni with a pass. Bertoni caught it cleanly and launched the ball across the box and into the goal.

The Argentine fans—loud, raucous, and excited throughout the match—went into a frenzy. The celebrations lasted for days afterward. At long last, Argentina was the champion of the soccer world.

CHAPTER TWELVE

★ 1982 ★

BIGGER THAN EVER

Twenty-four. That was how many nations would participate in the World Cup's newly expanded format. Soccer had grown so popular in so many parts of the globe that sixteen slots were simply not enough anymore. Those twenty-four teams were separated into six groups of four for first-round play. While many of the matches ended predictably, there were some surprising upsets.

The most stunning of these was the 2–1 defeat of West Germany by newcomer Algeria. The Germans recovered from the loss to beat Chile, 4–1, in their next match. The Algerians, meanwhile, lost to Austria, 2–0, and then beat Chile, 3–2. Chile was out, having lost to Austria earlier in the series, 1–0.

There was just one game left in the series, that between West Germany and Austria. The question now was, how would the remaining teams rank when that game was finished?

The answer would be decided in the final point

tally. Algeria had earned five goals while giving up five. Before the match, West Germany also had earned five goals, but let in only three. Austria had scored three goals and allowed none.

From these statistics, it would seem that Algeria would beat out Austria for second place unless Austria won against West Germany. But two of Algeria's goals had been earned during its "away" game against Germany. In the final tally, those two would count for just a little less than goals made during "home" games.

Both West Germany and Austria knew that going into the final match of their group play. They knew something else: if Germany won by a score of 1–0, then it would take first place in the group—and Austria, having given up just one away goal to Algeria's two, would take second.

With that in mind, the Austrians agreed to oust the Algerians by allowing the Germans to score the single necessary goal. That goal was scored ten minutes into the game. After that, both the Germans and the Austrians treated the match like a practice, pushing the ball this way and that while never really attempting to score.

The Algerians realized what was happening, of course. Like the Brazilians in the previous Cup, they cried foul. But there was nothing anyone could do at that point. FIFA eventually changed the scheduling of group play so that in future World Cups, games would be played at the same time. No team would ever again go into a final match knowing how many points they needed to advance.

Final score: West Germany 1, Austria 0—and goodbye, Algeria.

The Algerians were partly avenged in the second-round play when the Austrians came in behind the French and were thus eliminated from the semifinals. Germany managed to stay alive, however, squeaking out a 2–1 win over Spain and ending their match against England in a 0–0 draw.

Also reaching the semifinals were Poland and Italy. These two teams had met earlier in the tournament in a game that had ended in a scoreless tie. That they were to meet again now was something of a shock, for most had believed Italy would be eliminated in the second round by Brazil. But in one of the most amazing upsets of the competition, Italy won, 3–2, beating a team laden with talent. Even more amazing, all three of Italy's goals were scored by one player, Paolo Rossi.

Rossi was a talented player with a checkered soccer history. After a promising debut, he suffered from knee problems and was let go by his team, Juventus. He recovered, however, and grew into a capable player who often slammed home big goals. Although not a standout then, he helped Italy to the World Cup in 1978. Soon afterward, trouble found him again. He and several other players were accused of fixing matches. Rossi was never found guilty, but he was suspended from soccer for two years nonetheless. He came back just in time to take part in the 1982 World Cup.

His return to the international tournament had many people muttering in dismay. Rossi may have been good once, but now?

Rossi turned those mutters into cheers in the second-round Brazil-Italy match. He scored five minutes into that game. Twenty minutes later, he broke a tie to give Italy a one-goal advantage. And in the seventy-fourth minute, he broke a *second* tie to give Italy the win!

That victory was by far Italy's most electrifying. And Rossi wasn't done yet. He scored both of Italy's goals in its 2–0 win over Poland, earning his team a shot at the championship title!

To get that title, Italy would have to beat West Germany. The Germans weren't about to go down without a fight, as they'd shown in their semifinal match against France; that game left one French player unconscious when the German goalkeeper plowed into him. It was also the first semifinal to be decided by a penalty shoot-out. Germany managed to put one goal more into the net than France to take its place on the pitch with Italy.

Italy entered the finals as the crowd favorites. Germany, on the other hand, found itself the object of jeers from people who felt the team had cheated Algeria in the earlier round. Perhaps the negative vibe affected the Germans, or maybe they were still exhausted from the grueling game against France.

Whatever the cause, Germany simply couldn't hold its own against the Italian attack. The first half ended without a score. Then, at the start of the second, Rossi plugged one into the net, his sixth consecutive goal and the team's first of the game. Twelve minutes later, teammate Marco Tardelli booted in the second. When Alessandro Altobelli blasted in a third, the game was in Italy's pocket.

Not even a late-game goal by Paul Breitner could dampen the Italians' enthusiasm. Tardelli summed up his teammates' joy with a wild, fist-pumping romp around the pitch. With that victory, Italy joined Brazil as the second team to win three championships!

CHAPTER THIRTEEN
★ 1986 ★
"THE HAND OF GOD"

The thirteenth World Cup tournament almost didn't have a host. Colombia had originally been selected, but two years before the competition was to begin, the government announced that it didn't have the money to foot the bills. The United States, Canada, and Mexico all put in bids to take Colombia's place. Mexico won, becoming the first country to host two World Cups.

Natural disaster nearly prevented Mexico from assuming that role, however. On September 19, 1985, residents of Mexico City were shaken from their beds by a devastating earthquake. Buildings collapsed, leaving thousands dead and hundreds of thousands homeless. Pipes that transported drinking water were in disrepair for weeks. Electricity, communications, transportation, and other services were also cut off. Hospitals were overrun with injured.

Amazingly, the stadiums dotting the surrounding areas were unaffected. When FIFA contacted

Mexico's government with an offer to find a new host country, the authorities insisted that they could—and would—fulfill their role. Not to do so would be a further blow to their country's shattered morale.

In May, the twenty-four national teams that had made it to the final competition arrived in Mexico for the first round of games. The format had changed slightly from previous years; this time, the top two teams from the initial six groups would be joined by the top four third-place finishers for a sixteen-game knockout round. The surviving eight teams would then take part in the quarterfinals, with the four winners of that round advancing to the semifinals. As always, the two victors of the semifinals would then face off for the championship title.

There were three newcomers to the Cup in 1986: Canada, Iraq, and Denmark. The last of these proved to be one of the most surprising teams of the first round. Grouped with Uruguay, Scotland, and West Germany, the plucky players from the tiny Scandinavian country went undefeated to earn a spot in the round of sixteen! Their biggest win came against Uruguay; in the second half, they plugged four goals into the net for a game total of six. Preben Elkjaer was responsible for three of those goals, his team's first World Cup hat trick. Uruguay, two-time world champion, scored just once.

The knockout round was as far as the aptly nicknamed "Danish Dynamite" got, however. Spain trounced them, 5–1. But Denmark's meteoric rise proved once again that every team in the World Cup has a shot at the prize.

Morocco discovered just that. Like Denmark, Morocco was the unexpected survivor of the first round and, in doing so, became the first African country ever to advance in the competition. Unfortunately, its ride ended with a loss to West Germany, 1–0.

The round of sixteen produced some unforeseen upsets, too. Belgium outlasted the Soviet Union's one-man onslaught, a hat trick by Igor Belanov, to win in extra minutes, 4–3. France unseated the reigning champs from Italy, 2–0. And things got ugly in the Argentina-Uruguay match, with seven players receiving cautions. Luckily for the Argentines, their star player was not among those carded.

Diego Maradona had been playing soccer all his life. Too young to be part of the national team for the 1978 World Cup, he was added to the squad for the 1982 competition in Spain. There he booted in two goals in first-round games before his hot temper got him ejected for roughing up a Brazilian player. Now, in 1986, he was determined to show the world what he could do.

His first contribution to Argentina's bid for the finals came in the second game, when he booted in a goal against the Italians to tie the match, 1–1. He nearly added a second goal to his personal tally in the knockout game against Uruguay, but officials disallowed the point. Luckily, one of his teammates had put one in the net, so Argentina survived and continued on to the quarterfinals.

It was in this match, against England, that Maradona made two goals that have gone down in soccer history. Six minutes into the second half, English defender Steve Hodge lofted the ball into the air in an attempted pass to his goalkeeper, Peter Shilton. Shilton ran to make the catch, arms outstretched high over his head.

At the same time, Maradona raced to meet the ball. He, too, leaped high in the air, raising one arm as he did. It seemed unlikely that the Argentine would outjump the Englishman—after all, Maradona stood at just five feet, five inches, while Shilton was over six feet tall. But somehow, Maradona connected instead of Shilton. As the two players fell in a heap, the ball bounded into the net for Argentina's first goal!

Maradona leaped to his feet, shouting and celebrating. But interestingly, none of his teammates ran to celebrate with him right away. Film of the play shows the reason for their hesitation. Maradona had punched the ball into the net with his fist!

Maradona knew that the official had missed his flagrant foul. With no instant replay at the time, he realized there was just one thing to do.

"Come hug me," he recalled yelling to his teammates, "or the referee isn't going to allow it!" Only then did the celebration take place for the goal Maradona later dubbed "the Hand of God."

England must have been seething at the mistakenly awarded point. But there was no mistaking the goal that happened next.

Just three minutes after the Hand of God, Maradona received a pass from Héctor Enrique. He was just shy of the half-field mark. Three English defenders moved in—only to find that Maradona was no longer there.

Legs flashing, the Argentine raced down the field with the English players in hot pursuit. Two converged on him, but he threaded his way between

AP/Wide World Photos

The infamous "Hand of God" goal. Fist raised, Argentina's Diego Maradona (front) literally beats English goalkeeper Peter Shilton to the punch to make one of the most controversial goals in World Cup history.

them as if they were no more than orange cones set up for dribbling practice. He then cut toward the goal. Shilton came out to challenge him, but Maradona was simply unstoppable. With one swift and decisive kick, he launched the ball into the net. Goal!

The entire ten-second run displayed Maradona's incredible ability to outthink and outmaneuver his defenders. It is considered by many soccer followers to be the best goal ever made in the World Cup. That day, it was good enough to clinch Argentina's victory over England.

Argentina continued its run for the championship in the semifinals, where Maradona and his teammates dominated Belgium. While Belgium took more shots on goal overall, none of them managed to find the back of the net. Maradona, on the other hand, walloped back-to-back goals in the first ten minutes of the second half. That's all his team needed. Final score: Argentina 2, Belgium 0.

The South American nation was back in the finals for the third time in World Cup history. Its opponent, West Germany, was making its fifth appearance there. Both teams were packed with talent, but it was Argentina who landed the first blow.

Maradona, the obvious scoring threat, was being closely guarded. That left his teammate José Luis Brown wide open—and Brown took full advantage by heading a free kick over the German goalkeeper for the first point of the game.

The second point belonged to Argentina, too. This time it was Jorge Valdano who charged virtually unchallenged into the penalty box. One kick later, Argentina led, 2–0.

But the Germans hadn't reached the finals by lying down and playing dead. They rallied late in the second half and socked in back-to-back goals in just sixteen minutes. As the clock ticked down, the match looked poised to go into extra time.

It didn't, thanks to Maradona. With just seven minutes remaining in the final, he captured the ball in the midst of a swarm of German players and made a jaw-dropping pass to teammate Jorge Burruchaga. Seconds later, Burruchaga scored! And when the Argentines held on to their 3–2 lead, they had their second World Cup trophy.

CHAPTER FOURTEEN
★ 1990 ★
AN EMPTY CUP

By all accounts, the 1990 World Cup in Italy was the worst ever played. It was low scoring, with an average of fewer than three goals per game. Matches featured defensive "strategy" that recalled the days when Pelé was mauled on the pitch. Brutal hacks, vicious attacks, and slashing tackles resulted in a record sixteen red cards. With so much of the focus on defense, many games ended in draws; four of the twelve games in the final rounds were decided by penalty shoot-outs. Perhaps most telling of all, the second-place team scored just five goals on the way to the championship!

Fortunately, there were a few high points that lifted the competition out of the doldrums. Cameroon, a small African nation, proved the most inspiring—and one of its players, Roger Milla, became a fan favorite.

Milla wasn't originally slated to play for Cameroon. At thirty-eight, he was considered past his prime, at least by Cameroon's coach. The president of Cameroon disagreed. He insisted that Milla be added to the roster, for he believed Milla could provide the spark the team needed to succeed.

As it turned out, the president was right: Milla had plenty of life still in him. While he wasn't a starter, he netted several key goals coming off the bench. After watching his teammates beat the reigning champs, Argentina, in the first match, 1–0, he stuck in two goals during a hard-fought victory over Romania. He chalked up two lifesavers in the knockout round of sixteen, handing Cameroon a 2–1 victory over Colombia and a place in the quarterfinals—the first time an African nation had advanced that far.

But the quarterfinals were the end of the line for the sentimental favorites, unfortunately. After holding their own against England throughout regulation play, they lost, 3–2, in extra minutes when Gary Lineker blasted two penalty kicks past Cameroon's goalkeeper.

Penalty kicks made the difference for Argentina late in the competition, too. But it was an astonishing pass by the previous Cup's top player, Maradona, that boosted Argentina past the round of sixteen.

The match was against Brazil. Once known for its brilliant offense, Brazil had reworked its lineup in recent months to favor defense. There were now fewer players on the front line and a sweeper whose chief duty was to help protect the goal. Pelé, who was in the stands, remarked that, in his opinion, the new lineup was doomed to failure.

He was right. Brazil's concentration on defense left it weak offensively. And when its defense broke down, it was rendered powerless. That's what happened late in the game against Argentina. Scoreless through the eightieth minute, Maradona weaved effortlessly through a sea of hapless defenders and sent a brilliant pass to teammate Claudio Caniggia. Caniggia was all alone; one kick later, the Argentines were up, 1–0. Ten minutes after that, they were on their way to the quarterfinals—and one week and two victories after *that*, the team reached the finals for the second time in a row.

Along the way, Argentina literally thrashed the host country, Italy, in one of the most physical contests of the competition. Three Argentine players were given red cards for their abusive play. Incensed at seeing their players treated this way, many Italian spectators jeered and hurled objects at the Argentines when they entered the stadium for the finals against West Germany.

Such obvious disapproval of their tactics didn't stop Argentina from playing rough, however. In fact, one of their players, Pedro Monzón, earned the dubious honor of becoming the first to be tossed out of a World Cup final for his behavior. His teammate Gustavo Dezotti joined him later in the game after grabbing a West German player by the throat.

But by then, the match had already been decided. Not surprisingly, the single goal of the game was a penalty kick awarded after a foul by Argentina. Andreas Brehme took the shot, which sailed past the Argentine goalkeeper's hands. With that kick, West Germany recaptured the crown it had last worn in 1974.

CHAPTER FIFTEEN

★ 1991 ★

UNSUNG HEROES

With the conclusion of the 1990 World Cup, many soccer fans assumed they'd have to wait until the 1992 Summer Olympics in Barcelona for the next international competition. But they were wrong. In November 1991, a brand-new FIFA tournament hit the pitch: the Women's World Cup.

The history of FIFA's Women's World Cup is much shorter than that of the men's. It began with João Havelange, FIFA's president, who recognized that soccer had become as popular with girls and women as it was with boys and men. Following in Jules Rimet's footsteps, he decided to do all he could to boost that popularity even higher. What better way than to create the female equivalent of the most popular sporting event in the world?

FIFA tested the waters in 1988 with a two-week invitational in China. Twelve teams competed from the Union of European Football Associations (UEFA), the Confederation of North, Central American and Caribbean Association Football (CONCACAF), and other international leagues. Twelve became eight in the quarterfinals, then four—Sweden, Brazil, China, and Norway—reaching the semifinals. There, Norway edged out Brazil 2–1, and Sweden defeated the host team by the same score. The final match, played in mid-June in southern China, drew a crowd of more than thirty thousand spectators. In the fifty-eighth minute, forward Linda Medalen scored the game's only goal to give Norway the victory.

The tournament itself was a victory, too. Two weeks later, FIFA green-lighted the Women's World Cup.

Like the invitational, the first Women's World Cup (or the Women's World Championship, as it was then called) was a modest affair with just twelve nations competing. It was held in China in November of 1991. Incredible as it now seems, matches were only eighty minutes long because FIFA authorities incorrectly thought that women players couldn't handle the full ninety minutes.

In a field that included strong teams from Brazil, Germany, and Sweden, the surprise star of the tournament was the squad from the United States.

* * *

US coach Anson Dorrance went to China with one goal in mind. "We were going to win every single game and emerge as world champions. . . . This was going to be the beginning of a national dynasty."

In a team packed with talent, three players stood out: Carin Jennings, April Heinrichs, and Michelle Akers, known collectively as the "Triple-Edged Sword" for their scoring prowess. This trio was responsible for twenty of the team's twenty-five goals. Unbelievably, seven of those goals came in one game—and five of those seven came from one player.

At five feet, ten inches, with an unruly mop of long curly hair, four-time National Collegiate Athletic Association (NCAA) All-American Michelle Akers was a powerhouse in women's soccer. She put her considerable offensive skills to work in the quarterfinal match against Chinese Taipei. Her first goal came just eight minutes into the game. Twenty-one minutes later, she scored again. Less than five minutes after that, she put another one past the Chinese goalkeeper. At minute forty-four, she lined up for a penalty kick—and made it. Amazingly, she added one more four minutes after that!

"Five goals in one game. What soccer player expects that?" Akers said years later, a hint of incredulity in her voice. "I thought, 'I'm going to take every chance I have and score every goal I can and do whatever I have to to help our team be the best in the world.'"

The US team advanced to the semifinals against Germany. This time, it was Carin Jennings who wowed spectators by scoring a hat trick. Her three goals came rapid fire, in the tenth, the twenty-second, and thirty-third minutes of the match. Teammate April Heinrichs added two of her own in the 5–2 victory. The United States was in the finals!

Also reaching the finals was Norway, winner of the 1988 invitational and the US team's archrival. The two had met seven times leading up to the inaugural World Cup. Norway emerged the winner in four of those matches, including the last two.

"We always hated Norway," Akers later recalled (about the team, not the country!). "I loved hating them. It was great. For me, the more I hate, the harder I play."

Akers poured all her emotion into that match. Twenty minutes in, Team USA was awarded a free kick. Akers converted it into the first goal. But Norway's Medalen answered nine minutes later to tie it up at one apiece. The teams traded multiple attempts on goal, but with the clock ticking on, the score stayed knotted.

Finally, there were just three minutes remaining. Norway had control of the ball in front of its goal—or so it seemed until Tina Svensson passed back to goalie Reidun Seth.

The pass was bad. Akers swept in, captured the ball, dodged around Seth, and booted a shot into the unguarded net! The United States was up, 2–1!

"It's the goal you think about as a kid," Akers recalled of that moment, "and you're saying, 'Okay, last two seconds of the game, open goal, defenders are rushing down, the whole world's watching.' Can you score it? And I did it."

And when the clock ticked to the eightieth minute later, the American women had done what their male counterparts had never even come close to doing. They had won the World Cup.

Akers was awarded the Golden Shoe as the tournament's high scorer. Jennings received the highest accolade, the Golden Ball, given the top player, with Akers receiving the Silver Ball as the second best. Jennings also took home a Bronze Shoe for the six goals she'd contributed in the tournament.

Akers, Jennings, and the rest couldn't wait to share their victory with their fans back home in the States. There was just one problem: hardly anyone in the United States knew what they'd done. In fact, women's soccer was so underrepresented in the sports world that hardly anyone knew the Women's World Cup even existed! So instead of a heroes' welcome, Team USA was greeted by near silence when they returned home.

"We thought we had just conquered the world," recalled Mia Hamm, a future superstar who was then just nineteen years old. "And there was just one media person there."

Although the players were initially disappointed by the lack of recognition, they knew they had to put it behind them. After all, they had work to do—the next Women's World Cup was just four years away.

CHAPTER SIXTEEN

★ 1994 ★

A SHOOT-OUT—AND A SHOOTING

Since the first World Cup in 1930, soccer had grown into the number one sport on the planet. Its popularity outshone every other competitive game wherever it was played—with one notable exception.

For some reason, the United States had failed to give soccer a proper home. While other sports such as baseball, basketball, football, and ice hockey all had successful professional leagues, soccer did not. It wasn't that citizens didn't have access to soccer; in fact, with each passing year more and more children, teenagers, and adults were joining hometown teams. Creating a league from such a solid base should have been simple.

Instead, it took a push from FIFA for the United States to finally launch its own network of professional squads. When the United States put in a bid to host the 1994 World Cup, FIFA accepted, but on one condition: it had to develop a professional soccer league. The United States agreed, and two years after hosting the 1994 Cup, Major League Soccer was born.

The opening rounds of the 1994 World Cup began on June 17. Football stadiums from Foxborough, Massachusetts, to Pasadena, California, opened their gates wide, treating foreign visitors as honored guests. Contrary to what many other nations feared, these venues were packed to capacity every game with cheering American fans.

These fans were rewarded with a style of play that was much improved over the one seen at the previous, low-scoring, viciously defensive tournament. After 1990, FIFA passed rules aimed at encouraging players to score goals. To that end, winning teams in the first round would now be awarded three points instead of two. This extra point meant that players would be rewarded for trying to win rather than trying not to lose or simply holding the game at a tie.

FIFA also decided it was time to end a very dangerous move, the from-behind tackle. Too many players had been badly injured in the previous Cup to let such a practice continue. Now anyone caught tackling from behind would be ejected.

Another rule change was directed at keeping the

play moving. Before, goalkeepers were permitted to pick up a ball passed to them by a defender, bounce it a few times, and then boot it back into play. Now, they could handle passes from teammates with only their feet. If they didn't get rid of the ball quickly, a wily attacker could swoop in for the kill.

And finally, FIFA eased up on the controversial offside rule. Attackers would now be given the benefit of the doubt in a potential offside situation.

"When in doubt, keep the flag down" was FIFA's new direction to referees.

The rule changes were greeted with enthusiasm by soccer followers, including Pelé. "No doubt we will see more goals this time," he promised reporters.

Truer words were never spoken. The first round of matches had a huge jump in scores. One game saw a World Cup first when Oleg Salenko of Russia laid five of his team's six goals into the net!

That same match yielded another record, too. Crowd favorite Roger Milla—now forty-two years, one month, and eight days old—showed that he hadn't slowed down one bit in the past four years. He made Cameroon's only goal, to become the oldest player in Cup history to score.

Other players drew just as much applause from the enthusiastic fans. Italian Roberto Baggio, also known as "the Divine Ponytail," gave thrilling performances throughout the early round. But it was his second-to-last-minute goal and overtime penalty kick in the knockout game win over Nigeria that earned him a place in the hearts of thousands. Hristo Stoichkov of Bulgaria was equally astonishing. Behind his goal-scoring attacks, his team went all the way to the semifinals.

Two other players made headlines, too, but not for their outstanding play. After years in the limelight as Argentina's soccer hero, Diego Maradona was sent packing when he tested positive for banned drugs. Suspicion fell on him after he went into a crazed celebratory dance after a goal in the first game. Maradona had been caught using before but was allowed back in. This time he was gone for good.

The other player's story was much more tragic. In an early game against the United States, Colombian defender Andrés Escobar made a terrible mistake—he scored an "own goal," accidentally kicking the ball past his teammate and into the net. When the game ended in a 2–1 loss, Colombia was out of the tournament.

Ten days later, the disgraced Escobar was shot to death outside a nightclub in Colombia by a man allegedly enraged by the own goal.

Amid such tragedies, the Cup marched on. The US team managed to stay alive into the second round, where it played Brazil. Given the difference in the two countries' soccer history—Brazil was soccer mad, the United States just beginning to catch the fever—few gave the North Americans much of a chance. Some even predicted the Brazilians would be able to score at will against the less experienced host team.

That didn't happen, although the Brazilians certainly tried their best to make those predictions come true. They attacked over and over, forcing the United States players to fall back on defense and completely neglect their offense. In fact, the records show that they didn't attempt a single shot!

Despite the Brazilian onslaught, the game was scoreless for the first seventy-four minutes. Then, to the Brazilian fans' great relief, José Roberto Gama de Oliveira, known as Bebeto, finally pushed one past the US goalkeeper. The South Americans walked away with the win, although chances are they didn't feel like celebrating. After all, they had botched all but one scoring opportunity against a much weaker team.

Brazil was the only team from the Americas to reach the quarterfinals. The other seven were all from Europe. But anyone who predicted a European-only final was mistaken. Brazil beat the Netherlands and then Sweden, to reach the championship round for the fifth time.

Facing Brazil on the pitch was the powerful team from Italy. With each country owning three world championships, it looked to be a match for the ages.

It wasn't. After ninety minutes of regulation play, neither team had scored. The game was still deadlocked at 0–0 after extra time. For the first time ever, the World Cup would be decided by a penalty shoot-out.

Five players from each team were selected to kick. Italy, the away team, went first for the series of alternating shots. Eight shots later, the tally stood at Brazil 3, Italy 2.

Roberto Baggio, his leg bandaged because of a hamstring pull, went to the line for Italy. If his kick was good, the score would be tied, but Brazil would still have one final chance to go ahead. If he missed, however, the Brazilians would win without having to take their last shot.

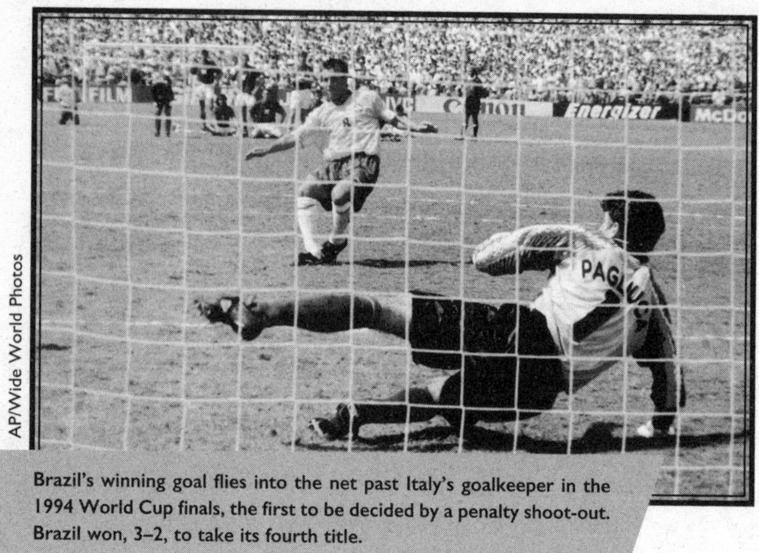

AP/Wide World Photos

Brazil's winning goal flies into the net past Italy's goalkeeper in the 1994 World Cup finals, the first to be decided by a penalty shoot-out. Brazil won, 3–2, to take its fourth title.

Baggio trotted forward, accelerating as he approached the ball. He drew his foot back and kicked. The ball soared high—too high! It flew over the goal's crossbar and into the field beyond!

Twenty-four years after its last victory, Brazil was once more on top of the world.

CHAPTER SEVENTEEN
★ 1995 ★

FROM RUNNER-UP TO CHAMPION

When the second Women's World Cup opened in Sweden in early June of 1995, Norway was still smarting from its 1991 loss to the United States. This time, its players were determined to emerge victorious.

They got off to a strong start in group play. In their first match, they ran circles around the Nigerian defense, for a blistering 8–0 win. Two days later, they took on England. Seven minutes into the match, Norway's Tone Haugen booted in the first of her team's two goals. Teammate Hege Riise added the second thirty minutes later. Meanwhile, Norwegian keeper Bente Nordby prevented England from putting the ball into the net throughout the ninety minutes of play. Final score: Norway 2, England 0.

Nordby was just as effective in Norway's third group match against Canada. Her teammates, meanwhile, drilled in seven goals, to give the Norwegians a 7–0 victory and an astounding three-day total of seventeen goals. Eight of those goals came from just two players, Riise with three and Ann Kristin Aarønes with five.

The United States started their group stage with a 3–3 tie with China. That match proved costly for the Americans. Just seven minutes in, Michelle Akers, superstar of the 1991 championship team, collided head-on with a Chinese player. The blow knocked her out cold, forcing coach Tony DiCicco to sideline her until further notice. Yet even without Akers in the lineup, Team USA defeated both Denmark and Australia.

The quarterfinals found the Americans surging past Japan. Kristine Lilly got things going with an early goal less then ten minutes into the match, followed by a second as the clock ticked toward the halftime mark. Tiffeny Milbrett volleyed in a third a few minutes later, a perfectly placed goal she celebrated by somersaulting on the pitch. Tisha Venturini drained the fourth and final goal of the match, to give Team USA the 4–0 victory and a berth in the semifinals.

Their opponents in that match? Their rivals, Norway.

The Norwegians reached the semifinals by handing

Denmark a decisive 3–1 defeat. They came into the June 15 match against the United States focused and prepared. "We didn't think about what was at the end of the tournament, but a lot about every match," Riise said. "What's the next step, the next step, the next step. And that way, energy [was] built up, which [made] it almost impossible to lose."

The Norwegians coupled that energy with an aggressive style of play. Other teams might have been intimidated by them, but not the Americans. They'd beaten Norway four years earlier and wanted nothing more than to take them down again.

Norway dominated play early on, but Team USA didn't give up. Then, ten minutes into the first half, the Norwegians were awarded a corner kick. Aarønes lined up near the goal. At five feet, eleven inches, she was taller than many of the other players. When the kick flew in high, she used that height to full advantage, heading the ball toward the goal.

US keeper Briana Scurry, who had made her international debut with this tournament, leaped and punched at the ball with both hands to deflect it over the goal. But the angle of the deflection wasn't quite right. Instead of sailing over the crossbar, the ball sailed just under it.

Norway 1, United States 0.

Team USA fought back, using every weapon in its vast arsenal. Joy Fawcett nearly tied things up with a blast that Norway's keeper just managed to push above the bar. But in the end, the Americans just couldn't put one into the net.

Final score: Norway 1, United States 0.

Team USA was devastated. Sobbing and embracing one another for comfort, they watched in dismay as the Norwegians dropped to their hands and knees to form a human train that marched triumphantly in a line before the cheering spectators. The train was partly a celebration of their win. But it was also meant to humiliate the Americans, for it symbolized the fact that Norway had just "derailed" their archrivals.

"It's fun to beat the Americans because they get so upset, make so much noise, when they lose," the Norwegian captain Linda Medalen said later, adding a piece of advice: "This is a problem. Never be weak."

Norway advanced to the finals against Germany, who had squeaked out a 1–0 win over China. Rain poured down in buckets throughout the match, soaking players, more than seventeen thousand spectators, and the pitch. It didn't seem to bother the Norwegians. They knocked in back-to-back goals in the first half, including one sneaked into the corner of the goal by Riise, her fifth of the tournament, for a 2–0 lead.

Germany couldn't answer. When the whistle blew at the end of ninety minutes, Norway was the new champion of women's soccer.

CHAPTER EIGHTEEN

★ 1998 ★

HOST HEROES

It may seem surprising that, given the number of nations in the world who vie to take part in the World Cup, many of the same countries wind up hosting the tournament over and over. But the truth is, the World Cup, like the Olympics, can be very expensive to hold. Money must be spent on promotion, on upgrading venues, on television and media coverage, and on making sure that the millions of visitors the event attracts can be housed, fed, and transported comfortably.

Still, it is an honor to host, and in 1998, that honor belonged to Jules Rimet's birthplace, France. World Cup spectators would be coming from more countries than ever before as the format had undergone yet another expansion. Thirty-two teams from the six continental zones would now have a chance at the ultimate prize.

As before, the teams were divided into groups of four (originally A–F, now A–H). But instead of the top two teams plus the best of the third-place ranks advancing to the knockout round of sixteen, only the top two from each group would move forward. After that, everything remained the same—quarterfinals to semifinals to finals.

There were a few surprises in the first round, such as the strong showing by newcomer Croatia, but even more disappointments. Spain had hoped to go at least as far as the knockout, but instead fell victim to an early slump and ended up losing in the first round. Team USA lost all three of its matches to come in dead last in its group. Cameroon, so strong in the previous two Cups, also failed to advance.

Another disappointment was England. The English players came in a close second place behind Romania in their group and hoped to overcome Argentina in the round of sixteen. But it was not to be, although they didn't go down without a fight. In the first half of the match, each team scored on penalty kicks. The tie was unraveled by a fabulous goal by England's Michael Owen. Taking a pass just over the midfield line, he raced down the field, dodged four defenders, and walloped the ball into the net.

"Splendida goal! Splendida goal!" one announcer raved.

Unfortunately, later in the match, Owen's teammate and international superstar David Beckham was sent off for kicking Argentina's Diego Simeone. With one player down, England gave up a goal—and when the game went into a penalty shoot-out, they felt Beckham's absence even more, failing to convert on two of their five chances. Argentina made four, to go on in the competition.

Meanwhile, to the great excitement of the home crowd, France was posting its best showing in years. They tied with Argentina for the greatest number of goals scored in the first round, and then beat Paraguay in extra minutes, to reach the quarterfinals. There, they knocked out Italy in yet another shoot-out, to move ahead to the semifinals.

Their opponents there were the Croatians, who had amazed spectators by coming out on top against Romania and Germany. They fought hard against France, too, but this time ended on the wrong side of a 2–1 score. The host country had reached the finals!

Facing France was Brazil, the defending champion and holder of four World Cup Trophies. Eighty thousand adoring fans crammed into the Stade de France in Saint-Denis knowing that, whatever the outcome, they were going to witness soccer history.

If Brazil won, they would vault to the top of the international competition as five-time champions. If France won, it would be their first victory. Either way, the match promised to be lively and exciting.

It was—for the French, anyway. Their star player, Zinedine "Zizou" Zidane, led the charge. At the twenty-seven-minute mark, he leaped above Brazil's defenders and headed a corner kick into the net. He repeated the effort less than twenty minutes later, converting another corner kick from the opposite side of the goal with another header. But it was the final goal—made by Emmanuel Petit in the very last seconds—that sent the crowd into a frenzy of joy, for it sealed Brazil's fate once and for all.

France, birthplace of soccer's greatest champion and World Cup pioneer, Jules Rimet, had finally earned the sport's highest award.

CHAPTER NINETEEN

★ 1999 ★

THE KICK SEEN ROUND THE WORLD

The 1999 FIFA Women's World Cup reflected the growing popularity of women's soccer. The previous two tournaments had showcased twelve teams. This time, sixteen teams from around the globe earned the right to compete. The teams were split among four groups, with the top two from each advancing to the knockout stage.

The three-week tournament was hosted by the United States and played in eight different venues with seating capacities ranging from twenty thousand in Portland, Oregon, to more than ninety thousand in the Rose Bowl in Pasadena, California. Television and media coverage was extensive, with all thirty-two matches broadcast live and more than forty million viewers tuning in to watch.

Not surprisingly, the media's primary focus was on the host team. And what a team it was! The Team

USA starting lineup boasted several standouts from the previous World Cups—Michelle Akers, Tiffeny Milbrett, Julie Foudy, Mia Hamm, Kristine Lilly, Joy Fawcett, Briana Scurry, Tisha Venturini, and Brandi Chastain, among others. These ferocious competitors had taken the sporting world by storm and captured the hearts of those with only a passing interest in soccer by winning Olympic gold three years earlier.

The sweetest victory of those Olympic games came in the semifinals against Norway. Team USA fought back from a 0–1 deficit to tie the game in the seventy-sixth minute with a penalty shot by Akers. The match went into a thirty-minute overtime, with the win going to whichever team scored first—a Golden Goal, as that decisive point was known. Ten minutes of play passed. Then midfielder Shannon MacMillan made her move, collecting the ball and cutting across the field on a diagonal. With one surefooted kick, she sent the ball into the net—and US soccer fans into the stratosphere with joy.

Those same fans—and thousands of new ones—had high hopes for their favorite team in the third Women's World Cup. The players were every bit as ready to deliver. "We are not here to lose," Joy Fawcett announced.

Team USA romped through the group stage, beating Denmark 3–0, trouncing Nigeria 7–1, and dispatching North Korea 3–0. In that final win, Venturini delighted the crowds by backflipping exuberantly after scoring the team's second goal. In all, the Americans scored thirteen goals and gave up just one.

The quarterfinals against Germany proved a little more challenging. Less than five minutes into the match, disaster struck. With the Germans pressing toward the US goal, midfielder Brandi Chastain got control of the ball. She was facing her own goal, so rather than turn about, she kicked the ball to keeper Briana Scurry so that Scurry could clear it.

But Scurry was in motion, heading far out of the goal to collect the ball on her own. She had yelled, "Keeper!" to signal her intention to come out, but it was too late. She made a desperate dive to stop the ball, but couldn't. The ball bounced and rolled into the empty net for an own goal.

Germany 1, United States 0.

Chastain was beside herself but did her best to check her emotions. "Soccer is all about mistakes," she remembered later. "I thought about my friendships and I thought about the crowd." And then she got back to work.

Milbrett tied things up ten minutes later. The score stayed knotted at one apiece until just before the last minute of the first half. Then Germany's Bettina Weigmann fired a shot from the corner of the penalty box. Scurry flung herself toward the ball, arms outstretched, but couldn't keep it from swishing into the back of the net.

Germany 2, United States 1.

The teams retired to their locker rooms for halftime. There, coach Tony DiCicco laid it out for them in plain language: "You've got forty-five minutes left in your dream. If you don't use this time wisely, you're going to go home."

Chastain took those words to heart. Just a few minutes into the start of the second half, Team USA was awarded a corner kick. The ball bounced off one player, then another, then landed at Chastain's feet. She didn't hesitate. Boot! One swift and sure kick, and the ball was in the net! Tie game!

Unable to contain herself, Chastain flung herself onto her back, grinning from ear to ear and holding her head with rapturous disbelief as her teammates swarmed her. The match wasn't over, but that goal had put them one giant step closer to their dream.

At minute sixty-six, Fawcett made that dream a

reality. With a graceful but powerful flick of her head, she sent the ball soaring past Germany's keeper. The Germans battled hard to try to tie it up, but when the clock ticked to the final minute, the score was the same: United States 3, Germany 2.

Next up: the semifinals against Brazil. The American squad drew first blood with a goal from Cindy Parlow just five minutes into the match. Akers made it 2–0 with a penalty kick near the end of regulation time. The Brazilians had failed to score even once. Team USA was in the finals!

There, they would face a very competitive team from China. The two teams had last met at another final: the 1996 Olympics. The Americans had come away with the gold that time, defeating China 2–1. They knew China wanted to even things up by winning this championship. But they weren't about to let that happen.

China's biggest scoring threat was striker Sun Wen, who had scored a hat trick in the second match of the group stage and two goals in the one after that. She'd also scored China's only goal when the two squads had faced off in the Olympics.

"If we can stop her," Milbrett remembered thinking, "we can pretty much stop China."

The teams met in the Rose Bowl in Pasadena on July 10. Close to one hundred thousand fans packed the stands. Millions more around the world watched on television.

China and the United States battled back and forth for the first forty-five minutes of play, but retired to the locker rooms having failed to score. Forty-five minutes later, the score was still 0–0. And, amazingly, after thirty minutes of extra time, that's where it remained—though China would have scored if defender Lilly hadn't made a miraculous save.

The 1999 Women's World Cup would be decided on a penalty shoot-out. Each team would have five chances to score in the kicker-versus-keeper nail-biter.

China won the coin toss. First to kick was Xie Huilin. She made it past Briana Scurry. Then Carla Overbeck faked out the Chinese keeper Gao Hong, driving the ball to Gao's left as Gao dove right. Qui Haiyan and Joy Fawcett made their shots, too.

Penalty kick goal count: China 2, United States 2.

Now it was Liu Ying's turn. As she backpedaled to prepare for her shot, Scurry bounced on her toes at the goal line, crouching and waiting to pounce. Liu ran forward and drew back her foot. Scurry darted forward. Liu kicked. Scurry dove—and knocked the ball away!

The crowd erupted. "Saved! Scurry!" a sports announcer bellowed as the US keeper hurried off the field, shouting and hammering her fists in the air with pure competitive intensity.

Kristine Lilly, up next, made her shot. United States: 3–2. Zhang Ouying got her shot past Scurry, to make it 3–3.

Mia Hamm, one of the most recognizable and beloved players in the game, strode onto the pitch for her turn. There was fiery determination in her eyes as she lined up her shot. She made it look easy, striding forward and blasting the ball into the corner to put the United States up again, 4–3.

There was one round of kickers left. "China must score here," the announcer reminded viewers, "or the United States will win the World Cup."

Sun Wen, China's most feared scorer, moved onto the field. She set up the ball. The whistle blew. She approached without hesitation and sent the ball sailing into the net behind Scurry's outstretched hands.

China 4, United States 4. The hopes and dreams of Team USA now rested on the shoulders of one player: Brandi Chastain.

What happened next is a moment that will live in sports history forever. Chastain placed the ball. When the referee blew the whistle, she trotted forward and kicked. A split second later, the ball rocketed past the keeper's outstretched hands and sliced just inside the left goalpost.

The crowd went crazy. Chastain, unable to contain her emotion, whipped off her jersey and dropped to her knees, fists clenched in victory and screaming with triumphant joy.

The United States had won the World Cup!

"I don't know if I can describe this in words," Chastain recalled years later with a bemused smile. "It happened very quickly, but it was in slow motion. But I could see it, almost see the ball not rotating and just hitting the back of the net.

"It was just ecstasy. It was joy. It was satisfaction. It was relief. It was exhaustion. It was awesome."

Awesome indeed.

CHAPTER TWENTY

★ 2002 ★

FIVE-TIME CHAMPS

The 2002 World Cup marked a break with tradition. For the first time ever, the competition was not held in either a European or an American nation, but rather in Asia. And, for the first time ever, it was cohosted by two countries, South Korea and Japan. This joint effort meant that three slots of the thirty-two openings were already filled, although due to a rule change, this would be the last time the defending champions were automatically given a slot in the Cup.

That left twenty-nine spots available to the 193 nations taking part in the qualifying rounds. Twenty-five of those nearly two hundred entrants were taking part in the competition for the first time; four of them—China, Ecuador, Slovenia, and Senegal—would reach the World Cup itself. Among the other nations participating were all seven previous Cup winners: England, Argentina, Germany, Brazil, France, Italy, and Uruguay.

Soccer followers buzzed with anticipation, wondering which, if any, of these seven would add another trophy to its shelf.

It wouldn't be France. With their best player, Zinedine Zidane, sidelined with a leg injury, the one-time champs bowed out in the first round after losing to Senegal and Denmark and ending their match against Uruguay in a draw.

That draw didn't help Uruguay too much, however. Those players, too, fell to Senegal and Denmark. They managed to place third in their group, but only because they scored goals during their matches—something France, unbelievably, didn't do even once!

The rise of Senegal was one of the big stories of the early round. The "Lions of Teranga," as they were nicknamed, roared their way past Sweden in the round of sixteen to reach the quarterfinals. Henri Camara was the hero of that game, scoring the African nation's first goal in the thirty-seventh minute, for a 1–1 tie, and then draining the winning shot in extra time for the 2–1 win. Unfortunately for Senegal fans, the tables were turned in the next match when their team lost to Turkey by a single goal after extra time.

The most exciting games of the first round were

played in Group F. This foursome was dubbed the "Group of Death" because the teams—Argentina, England, Nigeria, and Sweden—were all equally talented. Only two could survive the first stage, however, and after the six games, those two were Sweden and England. One of the sport's most recognizable figures, David Beckham, was the hero in England's defeat of rival Argentina. He booted in the only goal of the game, a beautiful penalty shot at the forty-four-minute mark.

Argentina's failure meant only four previous Cup holders—Germany, Italy, Brazil, and England—were left. But would any make it through the round of sixteen?

It was a close call for Germany, which needed eighty-eight minutes to score the game's one and only goal against the surprisingly strong underdog Paraguay. England won that same day, 3–0, over Denmark. Brazil kept its head above water in its match against Belgium with a 2–0 victory. Italy wasn't as fortunate. After scoring a fast goal in its knockout game against South Korea, the three-time champs couldn't hold the host country at bay. With just two minutes left, the Koreans tied the game and then took the win in extra time.

One down, three remaining. But would all three stay alive in the quarterfinals? Not a chance, simply because England and Brazil were pitted against each other in the first game. There could be just one winner, and that day belonged to Brazil.

The match started well for England. Midway through the first half, Michael Owen sprinted free down the left side of the pitch, received a cross pass from Emile Heskey, and outran Brazilian defender Lucio. Five steps later, he blasted the ball into the net, past goalkeeper Marcos.

Brazil tied the game twenty minutes later, and then jumped into the lead at the fifty-minute mark. England couldn't recover. Brazil 2, England 1; England out, Brazil on to the semifinals!

Germany joined Brazil in the semifinal round by beating the unexpectedly strong team from the United States in a close 1–0 match. Turkey continued its journey as well by defeating Senegal. South Korea sent its citizens into paroxysms of joy with its penalty shoot-out victory over Spain. That Turkey and South Korea had lasted so long in the tournament amazed many soccer followers. The question now was, how would they fare against powerhouses Germany and Brazil?

Better than anticipated, was the answer. Korea faced Germany in the first game. It was a defensive duel from the outset, with neither team scoring in the first seventy-four minutes. Then Oliver Neuville got the ball and streaked down the sideline. Teammate Oliver Bierhoff ran parallel down the middle, looking for a pass. When it came, however, it was just behind him. He turned to chase it—only to find his teammate Michael Ballack already there. With a massive kick, Ballack sent the ball rocketing into the net. Goal!

The game ended fifteen minutes later after neither team scored again. Germany was through to the finals for the seventh time in World Cup history!

There, Germany would face its longtime rival, Brazil, which had set aside Turkey, 1–0. The single goal had come from the foot of Ronaldo Luis Nazário de Lima. This was the third World Cup appearance for Ronaldo (not to be confused with his teammate Ronaldo de Assis Moreira, also known as Ronaldinho or Ronaldo Gaúcho).

Ronaldo had been a member of Brazil's team in 1994 at seventeen but did not play. In the 1998 competition, he seemed poised for greatness. Leading into Brazil's run to the finals, he had booted in four goals and one penalty shot. Then, hours before the deciding match was to begin, something happened: Ronaldo's name was removed from Brazil's starting lineup. Even more mysteriously, it was added again just half an hour before the kickoff!

What was going on? Rumors about the star player buzzed through the soccer world. It was only much later that the truth came out.

According to his roommate, Roberto Carlos, Ronaldo had suffered a seizure sometime in the night. He was rushed to the hospital, where he underwent several physical and neurological tests. All came back with reports that he was fine.

Ronaldo declared he had no memory of what had happened. He also declared himself perfectly fit and eager to play in the final. But it was clear to most that the previous night's events had taken their toll, for he played a sluggish game that ended in Brazil's defeat by the French.

The press was not kind to Ronaldo in the years that followed. He suffered knee injuries as well, leading some to whisper that he was done. But he refused to give up. He worked his way back to health and onto the national team. It remained to be seen if he could work his way back into the hearts of Brazilians.

It didn't take long for him to do just that. In Brazil's quest for the crown, he posted five goals. In the semifinals, he added a sixth with a forty-ninth-minute blast just inside the penalty box.

"Oh, what do you say about that? Extraordinary!" a British announcer cried after the ball bounced into the net. "Every World Cup needs a hero and Ronaldo is one here!"

Brazil won—and the next day, Ronaldo was a hero again.

The game with Germany was played before a sellout crowd in Yokohama, Japan. Partway through the first half, Ronaldo threatened with a point-blank shot on Germany's outstanding goalkeeper, Oliver Kahn. To his and everybody else's shock, the kick flew wide. But the attempt had a lasting effect nonetheless, for it sparked Brazil to step up its attacks.

Kahn was too masterful for them, however—at least until the sixty-seventh minute. Then he bobbled what should have been a routine catch. That was all Ronaldo needed. Flying forward, he snared the free ball on his foot and kicked. Kahn made a desperate lunge from the ground, but he just couldn't get in front of it. Brazil was on the board, 1–0.

Twelve minutes later, that score had changed to

2–0. Again, Ronaldo made the shot, although much of the credit must go to his teammate Rivaldo, who faked a stop before letting the ball continue on to Ronaldo—who then blasted it into the net.

The Germans simply couldn't recover in the time that remained. When the final seconds ticked off the clock, Brazil had won its fifth title, the most of any country in the world!

"It is a wonderful feeling to have won this trophy," a joyful Ronaldo told *FIFA Magazine* soon after the win. "I used to visualize the trophy in front of my eyes and imagine what a wonderful feeling it must be to hold it up in the air. It was a fabulous feeling actually to hold it in my hands."

CHAPTER TWENTY-ONE

★ 2003 ★

BACK IN THE USA

FIFA originally named China as host of the 2003 Women's World Cup, with a scheduled start date of September 23. But that spring, a virus called severe acute respiratory syndrome, or SARS, was sweeping through China. Fearful that the athletes and spectators might come down with the disease and then spread it far beyond China's borders, FIFA chose to relocate the tournament to the United States.

The change in location aside, this World Cup proceeded more or less according to plan. Sixteen teams from six continents arrived in the States in late September for group play. After one week, eight of those teams returned home while eight moved on to the quarterfinals. Most of those remaining eight had been expected to advance. But one was a surprise.

After failing to qualify for the inaugural World Cup in 1991, Canada had made appearances in 1996 and 1999. Both times, they came in third in their group. In 2003, however, the team of young, hungry Canadian athletes—their average age was just twenty-two—came in second, beating Argentina 3–0 and Japan 3–1, while losing to top-ranked Germany 4–1.

In the quarterfinals, the knockout-stage newcomers faced China. The two teams had met eleven times in the recent past, and eleven times, China had won. Many anticipated a victory for the Chinese this time as well.

China's coach, Ma Liangxing, might not have been among them. Prior to the tournament, he'd noted that "the gap between teams is narrowing all the time, as traditionally weaker teams catch up with the stronger teams. The World Cup should see plenty of surprises."

It was Ma's own team that was surprised. Early in the quarterfinal match, veteran striker Charmaine Hooper of Canada headed the ball past the Chinese keeper, Han Wenxia, and into the net. But with eighty-three minutes left to play, there was still plenty of time for China to even that score or take the lead.

They didn't. In the upset in the tournament,

Canada defeated China 1–0 to advance to the semifinals. The Canadians were ecstatic with their victory. They had trained hard, and it had paid off.

China had trained hard, too—perhaps too hard, according to a statement issued by the team shortly after its defeat. The statement noted that their younger players, eager to make a mark in the tournament, had pushed themselves to the point of exhaustion leading up to the group stage. The statement also suggested that the team wasn't as strong as in prior years because it had fielded older players who had stayed on for the chance to play in one last World Cup.

"We are not the force we once were," the team admitted before adding, "We firmly believe China will rise again."

Unfortunately for Canada, its World Cup dreams ended in the semifinals when Sweden came from behind to win 2–1. Canada wasn't the only favorite that ended up out of the running for the championship title. Host team United States had made its way steadily through the competition, giving up just one goal in undefeated group play and then beating its longtime rival, Norway, 1–0 in the quarterfinals. Then, in the semifinals, Team USA hit a brick wall: Germany.

Germany had been knocking on the championship door since the first World Cup, when it came in fourth place behind the United States, Norway, and Sweden. In 1995, it lost to Norway in the finals and in 1999, suffered its worst showing yet when it was ousted by the United States in the quarterfinals. Now it had a chance to pay back the US squad—and it couldn't wait to take it.

The star of the German team was Birgit Prinz, a dynamic forward who had posted six goals on the way to the semifinal stage, including two in the final minutes of her team's 7–1 torching of Russia in the quarterfinals. Alongside Prinz was Maren Meinert, who, like Prinz, had felt the sting of defeat at the hands of Team USA in the 1999 World Cup.

But with returning players Mia Hamm, Joy Fawcett, Briana Scurry, and others from the 1999 championship team, the United States had power and experience as well. They had added strength with younger players, most notably forward Abby Wambach, who had scored Team USA's only goal in the quarterfinal victory over Norway with a leaping header off a corner kick.

The United States versus Germany semifinals

kicked off on October 5 before more than twenty-seven thousand fans in PGE Park in Portland, Oregon. It was a physical match right from the get-go. Germany scored first when Kerstin Garefrekes headed a corner kick from Renate Lingor. The ball hit the crossbar, then rebounded on a sharp angle past Scurry into the net.

The score stayed at 1–0 for the remainder of the first half. Fifteen minutes into the second, Wambach came close tying it up with an attempted header in front of Germany's goal that saw her body-slamming keeper Silke Rottenberg, who had gone up for the save at the same time. Not long afterward, Rottenberg leveled Tiffeny Milbrett, who had leaped in the air to control a long ball in the penalty area. Milbrett hit the turf hard.

"It's gotta be a penalty," the announcer predicted. After all, Rottenberg hadn't touched the ball. But unbelievably, no call was made. Instead of a penalty kick, which could very easily have been converted into a goal, the United States was awarded a throw-in.

The teams continued to battle as the remaining twenty minutes ticked onward. Then Prinz got control of the ball. She raced downfield with two US defenders challenging her. Scurry darted out of the goal, ready to make the save. But at the same moment, Meinert charged forward. She was wide open. Prinz threaded the perfect cross to her between her defenders. Meinert controlled the ball and booted it straight into the goal.

Germany 2, United States 0.

"Now you're talking miracles for a USA comeback," one sports announcer commented.

"A two-goal game, that is almost impossible for this US squad to come back and get two goals," a second announcer agreed.

And if two goals were *almost* impossible, a three-goal deficit seemed *completely* impossible to overcome—and in the third minute of stoppage, that's what the US players suddenly found themselves facing. In a reverse of their previous goal, Germany scored when Meinert passed to Prinz, who blasted it into the goal from nearly the same spot from which Meinert had scored minutes before.

When the clock ran out, the final score told the tale: Germany 3, United States 0.

The German team was elated. "After our defeat in 1999, it was a big success to beat the Americans in their own country," Meinert told reporters later.

An even bigger success? Their 2–1 victory over

Sweden for their first-ever World Cup win. Sweden got on the scoreboard first, when Hanna Ljunberg sneaked past her defenders and drilled the ball past the far post just before the close of the first half. That one-goal lead wouldn't last long. Meinert tied it up just one minute into the second half. The score stayed knotted through the ninetieth minute to send the match into extra time. There, Nia Künzer

Stephen Dunn/Getty Images

Mia Hamm heads the ball over Kristina Kiss of Canada during the third-place match in 2003.

headed in the winning goal—the Golden Goal—in the ninety-eighth minute of extra time.

As for Team USA, they finished in third place, defeating Canada 3–1. It was a disappointing conclusion for their longtime fans. For Mia Hamm and Brandi Chastain, that match marked the end of a storied journey that had begun twelve years earlier. With their combination of skill, energy, and charisma, these two amazing athletes had vaulted women's soccer into the mainstream in United States sports. Their play had inspired young girls throughout the country and beyond to practice harder, reach higher, and work together toward their common goal.

And now the best of those young girls were ready to take their place on future teams.

CHAPTER TWENTY-TWO

★ 2006 ★

THE HEADER THAT SHOCKED THE WORLD

One billion. That's how many people were expected to watch the 2006 Men's World Cup final. If only Jules Rimet could have seen just how far soccer had come!

The road to that final game was littered with fallen favorites. While Ronaldo returned in fine form, earning a place in the books by besting Gerd Müller's long-standing record of fourteen World Cup goals, he could not get Brazil into the finals. The South Americans were unseated by France in the quarterfinals by a single goal made by standout Thierry Henry.

Argentina was thwarted in the quarterfinal round, too, in a 4–2 penalty shoot-out won by Germany. England, likewise, was shunted aside in this round by a shoot-out, which yielded Portugal three goals to England's two.

Of the greats, only host country Germany, three-time champs Italy, and recent winners France lived up to expectations by reaching the semifinals. And then, following Germany's defeat by the Italians, there were just two.

Italy's journey to the finals had been nearly flawless, with just two goals scored against them. One of those was an "own goal" that left the inadvertent scorer, Cristian Zaccardo, looking shell-shocked with dismay.

But if anyone expected Zaccardo's teammates to shun him for his error, they were mistaken. This Italian team had more camaraderie than any in recent soccer history, and it showed in every game they played. While there were standouts, to be sure, those players never put individual achievements ahead of their main goal—namely, winning the championship.

"If we really play as a team, as we know we can," Alessandro Del Piero commented in the days before the match, "then we can win."

Anchored by their goalkeeper Gianluigi Buffon, the Italians were one of the most balanced of any team in the tournament. With equal parts defensive might, outstanding midfield coverage, and offensive power, Italy boasted a combination that looked ripe for victory.

Of course, the French had their strengths, too, which led them to the final round. Chief among those strengths was their superstar, Zinedine Zidane, who at the age of thirty-three gave energetic performances game after game.

The two teams met in the historic Olympiastadion in Berlin for the finals. Nearly seventy thousand spectators filled the stands; millions in countries around the world tuned in at all hours to watch live coverage of the match.

The French struck first with a thunderous penalty kick by Zidane. The Italians answered soon afterward with a header by Marco Materazzi on a corner kick. That's where the score stayed as minute after minute ticked by. Zidane nearly got France up by one with a header of his own. But just before the ball sailed under the crossbar, goalkeeper Buffon tipped it up and out with his fingertips.

Had Zidane's header gone in, it would have been the talk of the tournament. Instead, it was a different header by the Frenchman that had tongues wagging.

The score stayed knotted until the end of the second half, forcing the game into extra time. Twenty minutes into that time, Zidane made a move on Materazzi. But the move wasn't aimed at the ball—it was a headbutt aimed at Materazzi himself!

What exactly happened before Zidane drilled his

shaven head into Materazzi's chest? Film shows that the two were walking down the field side by side, apparently exchanging words. Materazzi seemed to tug at Zidane's shirt. Then Zidane quickened his pace and got ahead of Materazzi. Suddenly, he spun about and—*wham!*—slammed Materazzi with a massive headbutt.

Materazzi fell like a ton of bricks. The referee ran over, whipped out a red card, and waved it over Zidane. Zidane was ejected!

In later interviews, Zidane claimed that Materazzi had been insulting members of his family and that's why he attacked him. Materazzi himself has remained silent on the incident.

The game resumed minus Zidane. Neither team managed to score before the time ended. As in 1994, the match would be decided by a best-of-five penalty shoot-out.

Italy took the first kick. It was good. So was France's first attempt. Italy made its second as well. On France's next kick, disaster struck. Goalkeeper Buffon stared at David Trezeguet. Trezeguet took three steps and kicked. Buffon hurled himself toward the lower left corner of the net—but the ball flew high and to the right, a sure goal!

Except it wasn't. Incredibly, the ball struck the crossbar and cannoned straight down, just outside the line. No good!

If the Italians could make the rest of their shots, they would be the winners of World Cup 2006.

That's just what happened. When Fabio Grosso blasted the final kick past goalkeeper Fabien Barthez's reaching hands, the Italian players went insane with joy. "I knew if we scored our first penalty, we could score them all," Italian coach Marcello Lippi said, rejoicing.

And with them all, the Italians were once again world champions!

CHAPTER TWENTY-THREE

★ 2007 ★

TWO-TIME CHAMPS

Sixteen years after hosting the first Women's World Cup, China once again stepped into the role of host to welcome teams from sixteen nations to their country. The field included the usual powerhouses of Germany, the United States, China, Sweden, and Norway, but also squads who were slowly but surely growing in strength.

Among this last group was the team from England. After failing to qualify in 1991, 1999, and 2003, the Brits surprised many soccer fans by not only reaching the group stage but earning second place in a tough foursome of Japan, Argentina, and the reigning world champs, Germany. Even more astounding was the fact that they prevented Germany from scoring a single goal when the two met! England didn't score, either, but that tie still put it one notch above Japan—and landed it a berth in the knockout round.

There, they faced the United States in the quarterfinals. As usual, the US roster was packed with talent. Some, like keeper Briana Scurry and Kristine Lilly, were experienced veterans looking to win one more World Cup before retiring. Other players were putting on the Team USA colors for the first or second time. But while they might have been young, that crop of newcomers had grown up watching superstars Mia Hamm, Julie Foudy, Brandi Chastain, and Michelle Akers redefine United States soccer. They stepped on the pitch ready to further the legacy those players had started.

They got off to a good start by winning their group. And they continued in the quarterfinals with a 3–0 win that dashed England's hopes of winning its first World Cup championship. Next up for the United States: Brazil.

The South American team had participated in every World Cup. They came in third in 1999 and reached the quarterfinals in 2003. In 2004, they battled with the United States for the gold medal at the Summer Olympics, ultimately losing 1–2 when Abby Wambach headed in a Golden Goal in the eighth minute of extra time. To say Brazil wanted to beat the United States in this semifinal match would have been an understatement.

Team USA wanted to win, too, of course. And

coach Greg Ryan believed he had the key to such a victory. Forty-eight hours before the match, he replaced keeper Hope Solo with Briana Scurry. The reason for the change, he said, was because Scurry had faced the Brazilians many times before. Scurry understood their style of play and, he believed, would be able to anticipate their moves better than Solo.

The roster change infuriated Solo. She had been playing brilliantly, producing shutouts in the last four matches. As far as she was concerned, being yanked from the semifinal starting lineup wasn't just insulting, it made no sense.

With Solo steaming on the bench, Scurry and her teammates hurried onto the pitch for the match. They looked as strong as ever, with Lilly nearly knocking in a goal just fifteen seconds into the first minute of play. Five minutes later, Shannon Boxx almost scored on a header.

But the Brazilians were equally strong, testing Scurry and the defense several times in the first twenty minutes. Near that twenty-minute mark, Brazil took a corner kick. The ball soared toward the near post. Had a Brazilian player been anywhere near it, she might have knocked it in for a goal.

Instead, it was US midfielder Leslie Osborne who

got to it first. She dove to make the save. But she must have misjudged where the ball would be, for instead of clearing it, she headed it into net for an own goal.

Brazil 1, United States 0.

Brazil scored again seven minutes later. Making the goal was their star player, Marta Vieira da Silva, better known as Marta. She captured the ball near the US goal and, dribbling with finesse and speed, cut through the US defenders and fired. Scurry got a hand on it, but it wasn't enough.

Brazil 2, United States 0.

There was still plenty of time for the United States to recover. But then disaster struck. Earlier in the match, Shannon Boxx had been yellow-carded for aggressively tripping a Brazilian player. At minute forty-eight, she collided with another opponent. Their legs tangled up and they went down in a heap. In what some viewers considered a highly controversial call, the referee flashed another yellow card over Boxx—and then a red card. Boxx was ejected. The United States would have to finish the match down one player.

Boxx's ejection seemed to take the fight out of Team USA. Brazil, meanwhile, took full advantage of the lopsided player count and used its speed, agility, and power to double its number of goals.

Final score: Brazil 4, United States 0.

The US players were gutted by the loss, though most conceded that Brazil had deserved the win. "They were beating us to the ball," team captain Lilly admitted later. "They had the momentum going their way. We were just trying to keep our heads above water."

On the bus ride back to their hotel, the tight-knit group of women did their best to console one another. But they soon learned that one player had chosen to point the finger of blame instead.

"[Starting Scurry] was the wrong decision," Solo had told a reporter immediately after the match. "And I think anybody that knows anything about the game knows that. There's no doubt in my mind that I would have made those saves. And the fact of the matter is, it's not 2004 anymore."

To her teammates, Solo seemed to be laying the loss at Scurry's feet, and those comments did not go over well with them. Many demanded she apologize. Others simply shunned her. Solo insisted her intent was to call out Coach Ryan for his decision, not to insult Scurry. But her defense sounded hollow to most ears. As punishment for her backbiting words, Solo was benched for the next match, which would determine third place.

The United States went on to win that match, besting longtime rivals Norway 4–1. Germany, meanwhile, rolled over Brazil 2–0 to win its second consecutive World Cup—the first back-to-back championships in the event's short history. When asked how she and her teammates planned to celebrate, German keeper Nadine Angerer had the perfect answer: "We'll party till we drop!"

CHAPTER TWENTY-FOUR

★ 2010 ★

PLAYING DIRTY

The 2010 World Cup was played in South Africa, the first time the tournament had been held in an African nation. Knowing the eyes of the world would be upon the athletes for the monthlong event, FIFA president Sepp Blatter made an appeal to the teams: "We want to prove that football is more than just kicking a ball, but has social and cultural value. So we ask the players to please observe fair play so they will be an example for the rest of the world."

Thirty-two teams qualified for the tournament. Group play whittled that number in half. The round of sixteen featured powerful play by the top teams—and also saw two controversial calls that turned the tide in two matches.

The first was in the contest between Germany and England. Germany scored first when striker Miroslav Klose helped a long arcing goal kick from his keeper, Manuel Neuer, reach the back of England's net. Lukas

Podolski made it 2–0 at the thirty-two-minute mark, but five minutes later, England's Matthew Upson closed the gap with a pinpoint accurate header.

The two teams battled for the next seven minutes. Then Frank Lampard of England got his foot on the ball in front of Germany's goal. He launched a powerful kick. The ball hit the crossbar and ricocheted down at an angle beside Neuer. Lampard, his teammates, fans in the stadium, sports announcers, and even viewers at home were certain the ball had hit the grass inside the goal and that England was now tied with Germany.

Neuer didn't treat it like a goal, however. Instead, he scooped up the ball and immediately put it back in play. The referees followed his lead, disallowing Lampard's goal—much to Lampard and his teammates' shock.

Instant replay ultimately proved that the ball had, in fact, landed inside the goal line, but not until well after the game. Neuer later confessed he knew it was a goal, but chose to act as if it wasn't. FIFA eventually apologized to Lampard, but it was hollow comfort for England's fans, many of whom still wonder if England would have beaten Germany had the right call been made.

As for Lampard, he claims to be over his disappointment, telling reporters in a recent interview, “I can’t see much point in having sleepless nights about it.”

On the plus side, that missed call was a loud wake-up call for FIFA about the need for equipment to help decide too-close-to-call goals. FIFA listened and, in 2012, began using goal-line technology.

The second missed call came in the match between Argentina and Mexico. Twenty-five minutes into play, Argentine player Lionel Messi lofted the ball to teammate Carlos Tevez. Tevez headed the ball directly into the net. Goal!

Except it shouldn’t have been, for there were no defenders between Tevez and the goal when he received the ball. That meant Tevez was offside when he headed the ball, so the goal should not have counted. But the referee didn’t catch it. Tevez later admitted he knew he was offside. Argentina went on to win, 3–1, to advance to the quarterfinals.

The eight teams in the quarterfinal round—Paraguay, Uruguay, Brazil, Spain, Germany, Ghana, the Netherlands, and Argentina—had all been at the top of their groups, with the exception of Ghana, which came in second by defeating the United States

2–1 in extra time. At the end of quarterfinal play, Ghana and three other teams had been eliminated, leaving Uruguay, Spain, Germany, and the Netherlands. The semifinals marked the end of the road for Germany and Uruguay. The final match of the 2010 World Cup would be between the Netherlands and Spain.

And what a final it was. The Dutch were well known for their aggressive style of play, but in the championship match, they took it to a whole new level.

"Ugly, vulgar," is how former Dutch superstar Johan Cruyff described his national team's approach, his disgust clear. "They were playing anti-football."

Spain gave as good as they got, however. As the game descended into a near brawl, the yellow cards starting flying—fourteen in all by the game's conclusion. There was also one red card but, incredibly, not for what many say was the nastiest foul men's soccer has ever seen.

The hit came at the twenty-eighth minute. Nigel de Jong of the Netherlands went for a high-bouncing ball. So did Xabi Alonso of Spain. In midair, de Jong kicked out with his cleated foot. But instead of connecting with the ball, he drilled his studs right into Alonso's rib cage.

"It was one of the worst tackles I have ever had," said Alonso later. "I have probably broken a rib. One of the most painful tackles in my life."

But if the Dutch players' intent was to intimidate their Spanish opponents with such punishing play, the plan backfired. With the match scoreless at the end of ninety minutes, the game went into extra time. Nineteen minutes later, Dutchman John Heitinga blatantly fouled Andrés Iniesta, earning him his second yellow card. That card was immediately followed by a red card, and Heitinga was ejected.

That left the Netherlands down a player, and Spain used their advantage to the fullest. They weaved downfield, passing the ball with short, sharp shots. Iniesta broke free—just for a split second, but long enough for his teammate to send him the ball. A Dutch defender charged to stop him, but he was too late. Iniesta drilled the ball into the net for a goal and Spain's first-ever World Cup win.

In Johan Cruyff's opinion, his countrymen got what they deserved for their dirty play. "Holland chose an ugly path to aim for the title," he commented. "But they ended up losing."

CHAPTER TWENTY-FIVE

★ 2011 ★

RISING FROM THE RUINS

On March 11, 2011, northeastern Japan was hit by a magnitude 9 earthquake. Japan is crisscrossed with fault lines—areas where the earth's tectonic plates meet and shift—and so is no stranger to quakes. But this one was far worse than any experienced in the island nation's history. It was so powerful that countries as far away as Norway felt the tremors.

As bad as the earthquake was, the enormous tsunami the quake unleashed was even worse. The massive thirty-foot wall of water inundated the northeastern part of the country, destroying everything in its path and leaving more than twenty-two thousand dead or missing.

In the grim reality that followed the devastation, playing in a soccer tournament seemed almost ludicrous. But four months later, the Japanese team packed up their gear and headed to Germany to participate in the 2011 Women's World Cup. The players and coaches recognized that Japan needed something positive to bring light back into their lives. They hoped that they could provide that light with a good showing at the championship.

Japan had a strong start in the group stage, coming in a close second behind England. In the knockout round, it faced the host country and reigning champs, Germany. In a side-by-side comparison, Germany was the odds-on favorite. It had walked away victorious in its eight previous meetings with Japan. Additionally, Germany had gone undefeated in its last fifteen World Cup matches (fourteen wins and one draw), had reached the semifinals in all but one World Cup, and had the advantage of playing before a hometown crowd. It was easy to see why it was favored to win.

But while Germany had statistics on its side, the Japanese players were the emotional favorites, the underdogs representing a country that was still suffering from its recent catastrophe. The Japanese had determination on their side—as well as a good deal of talent. As for stats, they could have pointed to their last outing with Germany two years earlier, which ended in a 0–0 draw.

At first, however, it looked as if the Germans were going to live up to expectations. They dominated the play in the first half. But despite several strong shots on goal, they failed to score. Japan, too, missed chances to get on the board. At the end of forty-five minutes, the score was 0–0.

That's where it was at the end of the second half, too, sending the match into overtime. In previous World Cups, the team that scored first won the so-called Golden Goal. But FIFA had suspended that rule in 2004 and returned to the original format of two additional fifteen-minute halves. If neither team scored during that extra time, the match would be decided by a penalty shoot-out.

In the first fifteen-minute half, Germany had a handful of opportunities to score. But each time, the ball soared wide or was blocked. It wasn't until three minutes into the second half that one of the teams finally got on the scoreboard. That team? Japan!

The shot was made by Karina Maruyama, a little-known player who had come off the bench at the end of the first half of regulation play. Homare Sawa, Japan's star midfielder, provided the assist. Seconds after the ball swished the strings, the two were crushed by their teammates in an elated embrace.

But the match wasn't over yet. As the final minutes ticked off, the Germans hammered the ball at

Japan's keeper again and again. Try as they might, though, they couldn't get it into the net.

Final score: Japan 1, Germany 0.

"I am so happy," said Sawa, who was awarded player of the match. "We have never won against Germany, and to do that at the World Cup makes me so happy."

The next day saw another nail-biting showdown, this time between the United States and Brazil. Things began well for Team USA when Brazil handed it an own goal less than two minutes into the match.

The Brazilians evened the score in the sixty-fifth minute, though the point was somewhat marred by a controversial call. Moments before, Rachel Buehler of the US team slammed into Brazil's superstar, Marta, outside the US penalty box. The referee awarded Brazil a penalty kick—and ejected Buehler for her overly aggressive foul.

Cristiane Roziera—better known as Cristiane—took the kick. The ball soared toward the open left corner of the box. But keeper Hope Solo dove out and made the save. The US players raced forward to swarm her, only to be stopped in their tracks by the referee's whistle. To their astonishment, the ref ordered the kick to be retaken!

No explanation was given, though in all likelihood,

Solo had moved off the goal line prior to the kick. This time, Marta took the kick. And this time, the kick was good.

Because of Buehler's ejection, the United States had only ten players on the field. Yet it managed to prevent Brazil from adding to their score. Unfortunately, Team USA didn't make a goal either. With the score at 1–1, the match went into overtime.

Two minutes in, Marta collected a pass and flicked the ball past Solo into the net. The United States had twenty-eight minutes to even it up. Try as they might, the Americans couldn't score. As the clock counted down to the final minute, the Brazilians were on the verge of the 2–1 victory.

Team USA denied them that victory with a stunning, last-second header from Abby Wambach. "It was a perfect ball," Wambach said of teammate Megan Rapinoe's high-flying pass. "It just popped over that defender's head. I was sitting on that back post and headed it in near post. I'm so happy it went in."

The United States took the match in a 5–3 penalty shoot-out that saw keeper Solo making an impressive save. Solo, whose ill-advised remarks in 2007 had made her teammates question her loyalty, was grateful to have helped, but deflected praise to her fellow players. "You can feel the energy and trust. Even when we were a player down and a goal behind in extra time, the team kept fighting. You can't teach that."

Both Japan and the United States won their semi-final matches, with Japan defeating Sweden 3–1 and the United States beating France by the same margin. The United States was back in the finals for the first time since its 1999 win. For Japan, it was its first-ever bid for the World Cup championship, and the first time a team had reached the finals having lost a match in pool play.

The US players took control right from the start, keeping the ball on Japan's side of the field and hammering shots on goal from different angles and from different players—Carli Lloyd, Megan Rapinoe, Abby Wambach, and Lauren Cheney, to name a few. Wambach nearly scored with a crossbar-rattling blast that bounced just outside the goal. But it wasn't until the sixty-ninth minute that the United States put the ball into the net.

The drive began near their own penalty box. Lloyd stripped the ball from Japan's Yuki Nagasato and sent it to Rapinoe. Rapinoe looked downfield and saw Alex Morgan. She booted the ball fifty yards in Morgan's direction. Morgan and a Japanese player gave chase. Morgan won. A few touches later, she laced the ball into the net!

United States 1, Japan 0.

Japan tied the game eleven minutes later, capitalizing on a bobbled defensive effort to sneak the ball past Solo. The match went into extra time. At the ninety-five-minute mark, Team USA took the lead again with a fabulous Wambach header off a pass from Morgan. It was her thirteenth goal of her World Cup career, a team record. But as the match clock wound toward the final minutes, Japan answered with a shot from Sawa that ricocheted off Wambach and into the net.

The score after extra time: United States 2, Japan 2. For the second time in the Women's World Cup finals history, the championship would be decided by penalty shoot-out.

Japan's keeper, Ayumi Kaihori, made two incredible saves and watched as a third attempt sailed high over the crossbar. Only Wambach made her shot, but by then, it was not enough. Japan outsmarted Solo three times.

Final goal count: Japan 3, United States 1. The Japanese were the world champs!

The Japanese players were beside themselves with elation. Not just because they'd won their first-ever

World Cup but because they'd given their devastated country something to be joyful about. "My girls played their hearts out," coach Norio Sasaki told reporters. "I'm stunned."

Throughout the tournament, the players had felt energy coming from the fans back home, but also from all corners the world, from people who understood the boost this win could give the suffering citizens of Japan. After their victory, the players showed their appreciation with a banner that read: *To Our Friends Around the World, Thank You for Your Support.*

CHAPTER TWENTY-SIX

★ 2014 ★

"A MIRACLE BOY"

Since the second World Cup in 1934, three teams had dominated the field: Brazil, which had won an astonishing five titles; Italy, which claimed four; and Germany, which owned three. Eighty years later, Italy had faded into the background somewhat, but Brazil and Germany still ranked among the best in the world. The two had faced each other in the 2002 final, with Brazil coming out the winner. Leading up to the 2014 World Cup, hosted by Brazil, many soccer watchers were predicting another showdown between the two powerhouses.

They were not disappointed. Brazil and Germany both emerged at the top of their groups with identical records of two wins and one draw, and identical goal totals of seven for and two against. In the round of sixteen, Brazil squeaked by Chile in an after-extra-time penalty shoot-out, while Germany bested Algeria in overtime. On July 4, the two teams won their quarterfinal matches, with Brazil vaulting past Colombia and Germany defeating France, to set up another epic clash of the soccer titans.

The match took place on July 8 before a crowd of more than fifty-eight thousand fans, most of them Brazilians. Brazil took to the field missing two of its star players, striker Neymar da Silva Santos Junior—or Neymar, as he was known—and captain Thiago Silva. That didn't deter the team's rabid fans from cheering and roaring for their home team. They believed in their squad and couldn't wait to see them demolish the Germans.

But their cheers died down a bit when Germany drew first blood with an eleventh-minute goal. They quieted a little more when Miroslav Klose, making his fourth World Cup semifinal appearance, knocked in a second goal twelve minutes later. But when Germany scored three more goals in the next five minutes—two from Toni Kroos and one from Sami Khedira—those cheers turned into out-and-out jeers.

In all, the German team scored five goals in less than thirty minutes of play. And they weren't done yet. In minute sixty-nine, André Schürrle scored his team's sixth goal—and he added their seventh and final one ten minutes after that!

With plenty of time left on the clock, it's possible

Germany might have racked up even more goals. But during their halftime break, the players had made a decision.

"We had to stay focused and not try to humiliate them," defender Mats Hummels told reporters after the match. "You have to show the opponent respect."

Brazil did manage to put one point on their side of the board just as the final minute of the match ticked by. The team left the stadium with the boos and jeers of their countrymen ringing in their ears and tears streaming down their faces. It was the worst defeat in their team's history, one they would never be allowed to forget.

"It is going to be horrendous for the Brazil players," predicted Danny Mills, former defender for England. "No matter what they do in their careers, they will be remembered for this forever."

The German players, meanwhile, were preparing for their finals match against Argentina, which had defeated the Netherlands in a penalty shoot-out. "We must enjoy what happened," Hummels said of their high-scoring win over Brazil, "but if we lose the final, this semifinal will not mean anything."

The 2014 World Cup finals marked the third

time Germany and Argentina had faced off in the knockout round. The first time was in the 2006 quarterfinals. The Germans won that bout in a 4–2 penalty shoot-out. They won much more decisively in the 2010 quarterfinals, four goals to none.

Their latest match was a battle from the first minute. Argentina had a golden chance to score in the first half when Kroos headed a back pass into empty space on Germany's side of the pitch. Argentina's Gonzalo Higuain collected the ball and raced virtually unopposed toward German keeper Manuel Neuer. Neuer charged out to meet him. Higuain fired off a shot—but it soared wide of the mark!

"What a waste!" a sports announcer cried. "He was presented with a World Cup final gift!"

"He obviously can't believe it," a fellow announcer put in. "He's absolutely, totally snatched by this."

Minutes later, Higuain had a goal disallowed when referees called him offside. Then teammate Lionel Messi missed a wide-open opportunity in the second half. Germany, meanwhile, hammered attempt after attempt at Argentina's keeper, Sergio Romero. Romero stopped them all.

At the end of ninety minutes, neither team had

scored. The match went into overtime. Twenty-two additional minutes passed. Then, finally, the scoreless tie was broken.

Twenty-two-year-old German midfielder Mario Götze had subbed in for Klose 2 minutes before the end of regulation time. Schürrle had replaced a concussed Christoph Kramer in the 31st minute. Together, Götze and Schürrle made magic in the 113th minute.

Schürrle got control of the ball. He dribbled down the left side of the pitch to far outside Argentina's box. Götze, being careful to stay onside, darted out in front of the goal. Schürrle saw him and booted a cross pass. Götze stopped it with his chest and with one smooth, continuous move, lashed out with his left foot, connecting with the ball before it hit the ground. The ball soared toward the far corner. Romero lunged to stop it. But the ball sailed past him and into the goal!

The crowd, the announcers, and the German players went wild. And when Argentina failed to answer with a goal of their own, Germany pocketed its fourth World Cup championship. Götze got his name in the record books for being the first substitute in World Cup history and the youngest player since 1966 to score a winning goal in the finals.

His coach, Joachim Löw, described his young

substitute this way: “A miracle boy. A boy wonder. I always knew he could decide the match.”

Götze himself seemed both elated and dumbfounded. “I just took the shot and didn’t know what was happening,” he said, before adding, “I’m very proud of the team. For us, the dream has become a reality.”

CHAPTER TWENTY-SEVEN

★ 2015 ★

MIDFIELD MIRACLE KICK

The popularity of women's soccer, and the Women's World Cup in particular, had grown exponentially since the inaugural championship in 1991. The 2015 World Cup, held in Canada for the first time, reflected that growth with an expansion from a sixteen-team to a twenty-four-team format. It also saw the first World Cup played completely on artificial turf—a fact that troubled many players. Turf fields are much harder than natural grass; they feared the injury count would be much higher as a result. Turf also holds heat much more than grass, and with the tournament taking place in the summer months, dehydration and heat exhaustion were very much a concern.

The twenty-four qualifying teams were divided into six groups, and each group played a series of games against other members of that group, with the top two teams from each group and the best four "runner-up" teams advancing to the new knockout round of sixteen. Alongside such powerhouses as the United States, China, Germany, Norway, and Sweden were first-timers Cameroon and Switzerland, as well as the defending champions, Japan. The two newcomers were eliminated at this stage, along with Colombia, Sweden, South Korea, Brazil, the Netherlands, and Norway.

The quarterfinal matchups featured an exciting head-to-head battle between Germany and France. France got on the board first when German defender Babett Peter accidentally headed a ball right to France's Louisa Nécib. Nécib took full advantage of the chance, delivering a pinpoint-accurate strike that swished into the net and sent the already enthusiastic crowd into overdrive.

Germany evened the score twenty minutes later thanks to a questionable handball call against France that netted its team a penalty kick. With just ten minutes left in regulation time, Célia Sasic stepped up to the line and calmly booted the ball into the goal. The European rivals were still knotted at one goal each at the ninetieth minute, and stayed that way through extra time, forcing the match to be decided on penalty kicks.

Germany went first and scored on that kick and the four that followed. France made its first kick, too, as well as the next three. If their last player, Claire Lavogez, made her shot, then the teams would continue trading kicks until one scored more than the other. That had never happened before in the World Cup—and it didn't happen now. Lavogez directed a powerful shot at open space, but keeper Nadine Angerer made a perfectly timed dive and batted it away.

Final penalty kick score: Germany 5, France 4.

The Germany-France quarterfinal wasn't the only exciting match of the knockout stage. Earlier in the tournament, the United States had come out on top of the so-called Group of Death—the name given the talented teams from the United States, Sweden, Nigeria, and Australia that made up Group D. Team USA defeated Colombia 2–0 in the round of sixteen in a surprisingly close match that could have been a much easier win for the United States. After all, Colombian keeper Catalina Perez had been sent off early in the second half following a collision with Team USA's Alex Morgan. But even down one player and with the backup goalkeeper in the net, the scrappy Colombians held Team USA to two goals, one of which was a penalty kick from Carli Lloyd.

Still, those two goals were enough to send the United States into its seventh consecutive World Cup quarterfinals. There, it dispatched China thanks to a spectacular goal in the fifty-first minute from Lloyd, who skied above her defender to head a high-arcing ball past the Chinese keeper's outstretched hands. It was her second goal of the tournament. She added a third on a penalty kick in the 2–0 semifinal victory over Germany. That game also saw her assisting on the second, late-game goal that ended the German bid for a third World Cup championship.

Coach Jill Ellis was proud of her team, but with the finals up next, she knew they couldn't rest on their laurels. "We will enjoy this tonight," she said, "and then our focus will turn to our next opponent."

That opponent, it turned out, was the team that had defeated them in the finals four years earlier: Japan. It was a rematch many soccer watchers had dreamed about—and many players, too, including Lloyd.

"I think we have really good momentum," she

told reporters prior to the match. "But I also think we need to raise our game. This is a final. This is where you put everything on the line, there's no holding back."

Teammate Abby Wambach, playing in what many expected to be her last World Cup, echoed Lloyd's sentiment. "I feel an air of confidence with this team right now," she said, before adding, "We don't overlook Japan for one second because they are a very organized and good team. . . . We know it's going to be a hard-fought battle."

Wambach's prediction was reasonable. The scores of the teams' prior matches in the Cup had been low, with most wins being decided by just one goal. Everyone expected this final to be a defensive battle won by a similar slim margin.

So many were surprised when, just three minutes into the match, Lloyd streaked into the penalty box and converted a corner kick from Megan Rapinoe into a goal. A mere two minutes later, that surprise turned to shock.

Lauren Holiday took a free kick from the left of Japan's goal. Julie Johnston back-flicked the ball toward the net, but Japan's defenders kept it from going in. Instead of clearing it, though, they bobbled it among themselves in front of the net.

Lloyd saw her chance. She slipped into the chaotic mass of defenders and, with one light tap, sent the ball into the net for goal number two. Less then ten minutes later, Holiday took advantage of an uncharacteristically bad header by Japanese defender Azusa Iwashimizu to give the United States a three-goal lead.

By this point, the packed stadium of fifty-three thousand screaming fans was going nuts. Three goals in less than fifteen minutes? Unbelievable!

Even more unbelievable? The United States scored again two minutes later—and again, it was Carli Lloyd who made the goal!

The point itself was perhaps the most unbelievable of all. It started when Japan turned over the ball on the US side. Lloyd got control. She dodged past defenders into open space. Unchallenged, she kept going.

As Lloyd neared midfield, Japan's keeper, Ayumi Kaihori, charged out of the goal, preparing to meet the attack.

The empty net was all Lloyd needed to see.

Without pausing, she delivered a powerful blast from the midfield line toward the Japanese goal. The ball rocketed through the air. Ayumi backpedaled, but not fast enough. As the ball descended, she made a desperate backward leap and got a hand on it. That tap shifted the ball's trajectory, but not enough. A split second later, the ball bounced inside the net!

Sixteen minutes, four goals—three of them by Carli Lloyd! She raced downfield, laughing and pointing triumphantly into the air. Her teammates swarmed her, their shouts joining those of the amazed spectators. It wasn't the only hat trick ever made in World Cup history, but was the fastest and the first ever in the final.

Team USA scored one more goal, this time by Tobin Heath on a perfect ball from Morgan Brian. Japan put two past keeper Hope Solo, but those goals were too little, too late. When the final whistle blew, the United States had won the World Cup 5–2, the greatest margin in the tournament's history. Not surprisingly, Carli Lloyd was awarded player of the match as well as the Golden Ball as the tournament's best player and the Silver Boot for her six goals.

Dennis Grombkowski/Getty Images

Carli Lloyd (#10) scores her second of three goals against Japan in the Women's World Cup Final in 2015 as a packed stadium looks on.

"I've dedicated my whole life to this," Lloyd said in an interview. "It took all twenty-three players to get this done, from the coaching staff to the players to our support staff. We all believed. We came here to win it."

And what a win it was.

CHAPTER TWENTY-EIGHT

★ 2018, 2019, and Beyond ★

From the first championship in 1930 to Carli Lloyd's 2015 fifteen-minute hat trick, no sporting event has provided more excitement, greater rivalries, or more stunning upsets than the FIFA World Cup. Qualifiers for the 2018 Men's World Cup have already determined the thirty-two nations that will be participating in the tournament, set to take place in Russia from mid-June to mid-July. Disappointingly for US fans, the United States national team was eliminated in the final round of CONCACAF competition. But there's still reason to tune in, for there's never a shortage of magic moments when it comes to the World Cup.

The 2019 Women's World Cup in France promises to be just as thrilling. With qualifiers ongoing throughout 2018, just which twenty-four teams will take part is still unknown.

But a few things at least are certain: The competitions in both the men's and women's tournaments will be fierce. The action will be electrifying. New heroes will be born while once-shining stars will dim. Unexpected upsets will delight soccer-crazed nations and doom others to disappointment.

While you wait for the action to begin, grab your ball and head out onto the pitch. Because you never know—with enough practice and determination, you might be the next World Cup superstar!

MEN'S FIFA WORLD CUP RESULTS

Year	Winner	Score	2nd Place	Host Country
1930	Uruguay	4–2	Argentina	Uruguay
1934	Italy	2–1 (aet)	Czechoslovakia	Italy
1938	Italy	4–2	Hungary	France
1950	Uruguay	2–1*	Brazil	Brazil
1954	West Germany	3–2	Hungary	Switzerland
1958	Brazil	5–2	Sweden	Sweden
1962	Brazil	3–1	Czechoslovakia	Chile
1966	England	4–2 (aet)	West Germany	England
1970	Brazil	4–1	Italy	Mexico
1974	West Germany	2–1	Netherlands	West Germany
1978	Argentina	3–1 (aet)	Netherlands	Argentina
1982	Italy	3–1	West Germany	Spain
1986	Argentina	3–2	West Germany	Mexico
1990	West Germany	1–0	Argentina	Italy
1994	Brazil	0–0 (3–2 PSO)	Italy	United States
1998	France	3–0	Brazil	France
2002	Brazil	2–0	Germany	Japan/South Korea
2006	Italy	1–1 (5–3 PSO)	France	Germany
2010	Spain	1–0 (aet)	Netherlands	South Africa
2014	Germany	1–0 (aet)	Argentina	Brazil

* Score of decisive match of round-robin final round

WOMEN'S FIFA WORLD CUP RESULTS

Year	Winner	Score	2nd Place	Host Country
1991	United States	2–1	Norway	China
1995	Norway	2–0	Germany	Sweden
1999	United States	0–0 (5–4 PSO)	China	United States
2003	Germany	2–1 (aet)	Sweden	United States
2007	Germany	2–0	Brazil	China
2011	Japan	2–2 (3–1 PSO)	United States	Germany
2014	United States	5–2	Japan	Canada

aet = after extra time
PSO = Penalty Shoot-Out